COLLECTED WORKS OF
PÁDRAIC H. PEARSE

COLLECTED WORKS OF
PÁDRAIC H. PEARSE

POLITICAL WRITINGS
AND SPEECHES

WITH SELECT POEMS

FOREWORD BY SAM O'HARA

ANTELOPE HILL PUBLISHING

"They think that they have pacified Ireland. They think that they have purchased half of us and intimidated the other half. They think that they have foreseen everything, think that they have provided against everything; but the fools, the fools, the fools!—they have left us our Fenian dead, and while Ireland holds these graves, Ireland unfree shall never be at peace."

PÁDRAIC H. PEARSE

GRAVESIDE ORATION FOR O'DONOVAN ROSSA
1st August, 1915

PÁDRAIC H. PEARSE

CONTENTS

SELECT POEMS

FOREWORD

The character of Pádraic Pearse haunts the conscience of modern Ireland more than it cares to admit.

A primary architect in the events of Easter 1916 and arguably the father of the Irish Republic, his historic and cultural legacy is surprisingly ignored if not outright maligned.

While Washington of Gabridali retain a place of pride in their respective nations, Pearse is even refused the honour of a stature by contemporary Irish elites.

An Ireland with one eye on the previous northern troubles, basking in neoliberal largesse is naturally apprehensive of a poet who trained child soldiers for battle, a poet who had as his life's goal the creation of a prelapsarian Gaelic nation by armed force and who was willing to sacrifice his life for it.

Intellectuals deride him as a proto-fascist relic and point to the intellectual lineage from Pearse to the Provisional IRA. Marxists half-heartedly attempt to claim him as their own due to his apparent embrace of socialism following his alliance with the patriot socialist James Connolly. The 26 county Irish state paid some degree of lip service to Pearse right up until the emergence of the Provisional IRA in the 1960s when it became expedient to marginalize him.

A segment of Irish Catholicism even accuses Pearse of *de facto* paganism, with attempts to create his own personal Calvary on the streets of Dublin.

Pearse exists to-day, despite his historical impact as a rather forlorn figure, misunderstood by an Ireland he thought could have had a much more radical future.

Only through a nationalist lens does the historical place and mission of Pearse become apparent, as well as why he presents a danger to the powers-that-be to-day just as much as in 1916.

Against centuries of the slow unwinding of Gaelic civilisation, and against the behemoth of liberal modernity personified by the British Empire, Pearse emerges as an almost quixotic figure. The very soul of Ireland was rotting in his mind. Not through British domination alone, but through the cultural devaluation generated by it.

Through his work as a Gaelic activist on the Western seaboard in Gaeltacht towns like Rosmuc, Pearse became infatuated with a living tradition typified for the Irish-speaking peasantry. It was this tradition, imperiled by the onset of modernity, that sought to eradicate residual elements of Gaelic culture through economic rationalization.

Against this seeming cultural death spiral, only an act of defense could nurture a genuine national rebirth, a concept at the heart of Pearse and his project. Born of mixed heritage to an Irish peasant mother and an English artisan father, Pearse played a salient role in both cultural and physical force nationalism of his day.

An accomplished writer and Gaelic activist, he spearheaded a radical brand of educational reform at his school in Scoil Éanna. Fusing traditions of Irish monasticism and Gaelic folk tales with the latest ideas in educational theory, many of his students would partake in the events of Easter Week. Defined strictly against the utilitarian theories of the British schooling model, the school played host to a radical testing ground for Pearse and his philosophy. It was an Irish-speaking school where boys were versed in the tales of Na Fianna, ancient aristocratic warbands that governed Ireland, and even practiced with rifles.

Further afield, the Ireland of Pearse's day was approaching a crisis point, the advent of a Catholic bourgeois in the 19th century propelling the prospect of Home Rule and awaking from its slumber the forces of Unionist reaction. The centuries-long process of Anglicanism was gathering pace with modernity, with the prospect of bourgeois nationalism in the form of Home Rule not addressing the root cause in Pearse's mind.

With the beginning of the First World War, Pearse reveled in the emergence of militant nationalism across Europe. With it came the prospect to smash the imperial apparatus governing Ireland and for a small radical vanguard to assert itself on the national stage.

Through the Irish Republican Brotherhood, a radical faction within the nationalist movement, he helped choreograph the Easter Rebellion in April 1916. Famously doomed from the start, rebels hopelessly took up strategic positions primarily in Dublin with Pearse commanding operations from the central stronghold at the Dublin's General Post Office. After a week of heavy street fighting and the destructions of swaths of inner city, Dublin nationalist forces surrendered unconditionally, with Pearse and other ringleaders executed soon after.

While initially derided as militarily incompetent, it triggered a remarkable volte-face in Irish public opinion. The rebels who were jeered by Dubliners as they were marched off to internment came home heroes only a few months later.

The Rising is very much as Pearse affair right down to the famous Proclamation largely written by the poet himself. What better way to respond to the malaise of Anglo-Saxon modernity than to mimic the heroism of Cú Chulainn on the streets of Dublin.

Famously, the rebels who hoisted the banner of the Irish Republic on Easter Week were a despised minority within a minority, scorned immediately after the Rising. The fact that Irish opinion flipped so easily to the nationalist cause is testament to the genius of Pearse.

Within three years, the political wing of nationalism Sinn Féin, trumpeting Pearse as their godfather, had won an electoral majority and felt confident enough to challenge the British Empire again by force of arms. Through the purifying act of self-sacrifice playing on primal Christian and racial archetypes, the folk spirit of the Irish was reawakened.

The execution of Pearse and other leaders catapulted Fenianism to centre stage and invoked an unexpected rebirth in national feeling across the country. Irish nationalists may have lost the shooting war on Easter Week, but they certainly won the spiritual one.

In the following volume, key tracts of Pearse's thought will be put on display: his segue from cultural into physical force nationalism as well as his ideas around educational theory. From his graveside panegyric to the veteran Fenian, O'Donovan Rossa, to his theories on Irish nationalism in "The Separatist Idea," a constant theme and motivating factor is his radical concept of Irish nationality, rooted in the blood and traditions of the nation at large. An eclectic thinker, he synthesizes a variety of concepts, even flirting with a national syndicalism in his essay "The Sovereign People."

For nationalists the world over, Pearse provides a template in the craft needed to prosecute a genuine national rebirth. He, like so many within the hagiography of Fenianism, deserves recognition as one of a select few who tried to reignite the spirit of nationhood across Europe n the 20th century.

Against the ersatz, Silicon Valley colony that Ireland has become, Pearse presents himself as a dangerous character. It is true that Pearse haunts the conscience of modern Ireland, and deservedly so. With the blood sacrifice of Easter Week, Irish nationality was reborn with a radical vision of what kind of Ireland could be asserted through force of arms.

Pearse and his project continues to this day. The Irish revolutionary polymath offers himself as a key figure for nationalists the world over to study and emulate.

Sam O'Hara
May 2020

Sam O'Hara is an Irish nationalist and activist dedicated to the preservation of Irish people and their distinct identity against the forces of neoliberalism.

POLITICAL WRITINGS
AND SPEECHES

THE MURDER MACHINE

PREFACE

This pamphlet is not, as its name might seem to import, a penny dreadful, at least in the ordinary sense. It consists of a series of studies of the English education system in Ireland. The article entitled "The Murder Machine" embodies an article which appeared in the Irish Review for February 1913. The article called "An Ideal in Education" was printed in the Irish Review for June 1914. The rest of the pamphlet is a collation of notes made for a lecture which I delivered in the Dublin Mansion House in December 1912.

P. H. PEARSE.

ST. ENDA'S COLLEGE,
    RATHFARNHAM,
      1st *January* 1916.

THE MURDER MACHINE

I

THE BROAD-ARROW

A French writer has paid the English a very well-deserved compliment. He says that they never commit a useless crime. When they hire a man to assassinate an Irish patriot, when they blow a Sepoy from the mouth of a cannon, when they produce a famine in one of their dependencies, they have always an ulterior motive. They do not do it for fun. Humorous as these crimes are, it is not the humour of them, but their utility, that appeals to the English. Unlike Gilbert's Mikado, they would see nothing humorous in boiling oil. If they retained boiling oil in their penal code, they would retain it, as they retain flogging before execution in Egypt, strictly because it has been found useful.

This observation will help one to an understanding of some portions of the English administration of Ireland. The English administration of Ireland has not been marked by any unnecessary cruelty. Every crime that the English have planned and carried out in Ireland has had a definite end. Every absurdity that they have set up has had a grave purpose. The Famine was not enacted merely from a love of horror. The Boards that rule Ireland were not contrived in order to add to the gaiety of nations. The Famine and the Boards are alike parts of a profound polity.

I have spent the greater part of my life in immediate contemplation of the most grotesque and horrible of the English inventions for the debasement of Ireland. I mean their education system. The English once proposed in their Dublin Parliament a measure for the castration of all Irish priests who refused to quit Ireland. The proposal was so filthy that, although it duly passed the House and was transmitted to England with the warm recommendation of the Viceroy, it was not eventually adopted.

4

But the English have actually carried out an even filthier thing. They have planned and established an education system which more wickedly does violence to the elementary human rights of Irish children than would an edict for the general castration of Irish males. The system has aimed at the substitution for men and women of mere Things. It has not been an entire success. There are still a great many thousand men and women in Ireland. But a great many thousand of what, by way of courtesy, we call men and women, are simply Things. Men and women, however depraved, have kindly human allegiances. But these Things have no allegiance. Like other Things, they are for sale.

When one uses the term education system as the name of the system of schools, colleges, universities, and what not which the English have established in Ireland, one uses it as a convenient label, just as one uses the term government as a convenient label for the system of administration by police which obtains in Ireland instead of a government. There is no education system in Ireland. The English have established the simulacrum of an education system, but its object is the precise contrary of the object of an education system. Education should foster; this education is meant to repress. Education should inspire; this education is meant to tame. Education should harden; this education is meant to enervate. The English are too wise a people to attempt to educate the Irish, in any worthy sense. As well expect them to arm us.

Professor Eoin MacNeill has compared the English education system in Ireland to the systems of slave education which existed in the ancient pagan republics side by side with the systems intended for the education of freemen. To the children of the free were taught all noble and goodly things which would tend to make them strong and proud and valiant; from the children of the slaves all such dangerous knowledge was hidden. They were taught not to be strong and proud and valiant, but to be sleek, to be obsequious, to be dexterous: the object was not to make them good men, but to make them good slaves. And so in Ireland. The education system here was designed by our masters in order to make us willing or at least manageable slaves. It has made of some Irishmen not slaves merely, but very eunuchs, with the indifference and cruelty of eunuchs; kinless beings, who serve for pay a master that they neither love nor hate.

Ireland is not merely in servitude, but in a kind of penal servitude. Certain of the slaves among us are appointed jailors over the common herd of slaves. And they are trained from their youth for this degrading office. The ordinary slaves are trained for their lowly tasks in dingy places called schools; the buildings in which the higher slaves are trained are called colleges and universities. If one may regard Ireland as a nation in penal servitude, the schools and colleges and universities may be looked upon as the symbol of her penal servitude. They are, so to speak, the broad-arrow upon the back of Ireland.

II

THE MURDER MACHINE

A few years ago, when people still believed in the imminence of Home Rule, there were numerous discussions as to the tasks awaiting a Home Rule Parliament and the order in which they should be taken up. Mr. John Dillon declared that one of the first of those tasks was the recasting of the Irish education system, by which he meant the English education system in Ireland. The declaration alarmed the Bishop of Limerick, always suspicious of Mr. Dillon, and he told that statesman in effect that the Irish education system did not need recasting—that all was well there.

The positions seemed irreconcilable. Yet in the Irish Review I quixotically attempted to find common ground between the disputants, and to state in such a way as to command the assent of both the duty of a hypothetical Irish Parliament with regard to education. I put it that what education in Ireland needed was less a reconstruction of its machinery than a regeneration in spirit. The machinery, I said, has doubtless its defects, but what is chiefly wrong with it is that it is mere machinery, a lifeless thing without a soul. Dr. O'Dwyer was probably concerned for the maintenance of portion of the machinery, valued by him as a Catholic Bishop, and not without reason; and I for one was (and am) willing to leave that particular portion untouched, or practically so. But the machine as a whole is no more capable of fulfilling the function for which it is needed than would an automaton be capable of fulfilling the function of a living teacher in a school. A soulless thing cannot teach; but it can destroy. A machine cannot make men; but it can break men.

One of the most terrible things about the English education system in Ireland is its ruthlessness. I know no image for that ruthlessness in the natural order. The ruthlessness of a wild beast has in it a certain mercy— it slays. It has in it a certain grandeur of animal force. But this ruthlessness is literally without pity and without passion. It is cold and mechanical, like the ruthlessness of an immensely powerful engine. A machine vast, complicated, with a multitude of far-reaching arms, with many ponderous presses, carrying out mysterious and long-drawn processes of shaping and moulding, is the true image of the Irish education system. It grinds night and day; it obeys immutable and predetermined laws; it is as devoid of understanding, of sympathy, of imagination, as is any other piece of machinery that performs an appointed task. Into it is fed all the raw human material in Ireland; it seizes upon it inexorably and rends and compresses and remoulds; and what it cannot refashion after the regulation pattern it ejects with all likeness of its former self crushed from it, a bruised and shapeless thing, thereafter accounted waste.

Our common parlance has become impressed with the conception of education as some sort of manufacturing process. Our children are the "raw material;" we desiderate for their education "modern methods" which must be "efficient" but "cheap;" we send them to Clongowes to be "finished;" when "finished" they are "turned out;" specialists "grind" them for the English Civil Service and the so-called liberal professions; in each of our great colleges there is a department known as the "scrap-heap," though officially called the Fourth Preparatory—the limbo to which the debris ejected by the machine is relegated. The stuff there is either too hard or too soft to be moulded to the pattern required by the Civil Service Commissioners or the Incorporated Law Society.

In our adoption of the standpoint here indicated there is involved a primary blunder as to the nature and functions of education. For education has not to do with the manufacture of things, but with fostering the growth of things. And the conditions we should strive to bring about in our education system are not the conditions favourable to the rapid and cheap manufacture of ready-mades, but the conditions favourable to the growth of living organisms—the liberty and the light and the gladness of a ploughed field under the spring sunshine.

In particular I would urge that the Irish school system of the future should give freedom—freedom to the individual school, freedom to the individual teacher, freedom as far as may be to the individual pupil. Without freedom there can be no right growth; and education is properly the fostering of the right growth of a personality. Our school system must bring, too, some gallant inspiration. And with the inspiration it must bring a certain hardening. One scarcely knows whether modern sentimentalism or modern utilitarianism is the more sure sign of modern decadence. I would boldly preach the antique faith that fighting is the only noble thing, and that he only is at peace with God who is at war with the powers of evil.

In a true education system, religion, patriotism, literature, art and science would be brought in such a way into the daily lives of boys and girls as to affect their character and conduct. We may assume that religion is a vital thing in Irish schools, but I know that the other things, speaking broadly, do not exist. There are no ideas there, no love of beauty, no love of books, no love of knowledge, no heroic inspiration. And there is no room for such things either on the earth or in the heavens, for the earth is cumbered and the heavens are darkened by the monstrous bulk of the programme. Most of the educators detest the programme. They are like the adherents of a dead creed who continue to mumble formulas and to make obeisance before an idol which they have found out to be a spurious divinity.

Mr. Dillon was to be sympathised with, even though pathetically premature, in looking to the then anticipated advent of Home Rule for a chance to make education what it should be. But I doubt if he and the others who would have had power in a Home Rule Parliament realised that what is needed here is not reform, not even a revolution, but a vastly bigger thing a creation. It is not a question of pulling machinery asunder and piecing it together again; it is a question of breathing into a dead thing a living soul.

III

"I DENY"

I postulate that there is no education in Ireland apart from the voluntary efforts of a few people, mostly mad. Let us therefore not talk of reform, or of reconstruction. You cannot reform that which is not; you cannot by any process of reconstruction give organic life to a negation. In a literal sense the work of the first Minister of Education in a free Ireland will be a work of creation; for out of chaos he will have to evolve order and into a dead mass he will have to breathe the breath of life.

The English thing that is called education in Ireland is founded on a denial of the Irish nation. No education can start with a Nego, any more than a religion can. Everything that even pretends to be true begins with its Credo. It is obvious that the savage who says "I believe in Mumbo Jumbo" is nearer to true religion than the philosopher who says "I deny God and the spiritual in man." Now, to teach a child to deny is the greatest crime a man or a State can commit. Certain schools in Ireland teach children to deny their religion; nearly all the schools in Ireland teach children to deny their nation. "I deny the spirituality of my nation; I deny the lineage of my blood; I deny my rights and responsibilities." This Nego is their Credo, this evil their good.

To invent such a system of teaching and to persuade us that it is an education system, an Irish education system to be defended by Irishmen against attack, is the most wonderful thing the English have accomplished in Ireland; and the most wicked.

IV

AGAINST MODERNISM

All the speculations one saw a few years ago as to the probable effect of Home Rule on education in Ireland showed one how inadequately the problem was grasped. To some the expected advent of Home Rule seemed to promise as its main fruition in the field of education the raising of their salaries; to others the supreme thing it was to bring in its train was the abolition of Dr. Starkie; to some again it held out the delightful prospect of Orange[1] boys and Orange girls being forced to learn Irish; to others it meant the dawn of an era of commonsense, the ushering in of the reign of " a sound modern education," suitable to the needs of a progressive modern people.

I scandalised many people at the time by saying that the last was the view that irritated me most. The first view was not so selfish as it might appear, for between the salary offered to teachers and the excellence of a country's education system there is a vital connection. And the second and third forecasts at any rate opened up picturesque vistas. The passing of Dr. Starkie would have had something of the pageantry of the banishment of Napoleon to St. Helena (an effect which would have been heightened had he been accompanied into exile by Mr. Bonaparte Wyse), and the prospect of the children of Sandy Row being taught to curse the Pope in Irish was rich and soul-satisfying. These things we might or might not have seen had Home Rule come. But I expressed the hope that even Home Rule would not commit Ireland to an ideal so low as the ideal underlying the phrase "a sound modern education."

It is a vile phrase, one of the vilest I know. Yet we find it in nearly every school prospectus, and it comes pat to the lips of nearly everyone that writes or talks about schools.

---

[1] Belonging to The Loyal Orange Institution, commonly known as The Orange Order, a Protestant fraternal order based in Northern Ireland, with chapters throughout Protestant Great Britain. The Orangemen politically and physically (forming militias) opposed Home Rule in Ireland.

Now, there can be no such thing as "a sound modern education"—as well talk about a "lively modern faith" or a "serviceable modern religion." It should be obvious that the more "modern" an education is the less "sound," for in education "modernism" is as much a heresy as in religion. In both medievalism were a truer standard. We are too fond of clapping ourselves upon the back because we live in modern times, and we preen ourselves quite ridiculously (and unnecessarily) on our modern progress. There is, of course, such a thing as modern progress, but it has been won at how great a cost! How many precious things have we flung from us to lighten ourselves for that race!

And in some directions we have progressed not at all, or we have progressed in a circle; perhaps, indeed, all progress on this planet, and on every planet, is in a circle, just as every line you draw on a globe is a circle or part of one. Modern speculation is often a mere groping where ancient men saw clearly. All the problems with which we strive (I mean all the really important problems) were long ago solved by our ancestors, only their solutions have been forgotten. There have been States in which the rich did not grind the poor, although there are no such States now; there have been free self-governing democracies, although there are few such democracies now; there have been rich and beautiful social organisations, with an art and a culture and a religion in every man's house, though for such a thing to-day we have to search out some sequestered people living by a desolate seashore or in a high forgotten valley among lonely hills—a hamlet of Iar-Connacht or a village in the Austrian Alps. Mankind, I repeat, or some section of mankind, has solved all its main problems somewhere and at some time. I suppose no universal and permanent solution is possible as long as the old Adam remains in us, the Adam that makes each one of us, and each tribe of us, something of the rebel, of the freethinker, of the adventurer, of the egoist. But the solutions are there, and it is because we fail in clearness of vision or in boldness of heart or in singleness of purpose that we cannot find them.

V

AN IDEAL IN EDUCATION

The words and phrases of a language are always to some extent revelations of the mind of the race that has moulded the language. How often does an Irish vocable light up as with a lantern some immemorial Irish attitude, some whole phase of Irish thought! Thus, the words which the old Irish employed when they spoke of education show that they had gripped the very heart of that problem. To the old Irish the teacher was *aite*, "fosterer," the pupil was *dalta*, "foster-child," the system was *aiteachas*, "fosterage;" words which we still retain as *oide, dalta, oideachas*. And is it not the precise aim of education to "foster?" Not to inform, to indoctrinate, to conduct through a course of studies (though these be the dictionary meanings of the word), but, first and last, to "foster" the elements of character native to a soul, to help to bring these to their full perfection rather than to implant exotic excellences.

Fosterage implies a foster-father or foster-mother—a person—as its centre and inspiration rather than a code of rules. Modern education systems are elaborate pieces of machinery devised by highly-salaried officials for the purpose of turning out citizens according to certain approved patterns. The modern school is a State-controlled institution designed to produce workers for the State, and is in the same category with a dockyard or any other State-controlled institution which produces articles necessary to the progress, well-being, and defence of the State. We speak of the "efficiency," the "cheapness," and the "up-to-dateness" of an education system just as we speak of the "efficiency," the "cheapness," and the "up-to-dateness" of a system of manufacturing coal-gas. We shall soon reach a stage when we shall speak of the "efficiency," the "cheapness," and the "up-to-dateness" of our systems of soul-saving. We shall hear it said "Salvation is very cheap in England," or "The Germans are wonderfully efficient in prayer," or "Gee, it takes a New York parson to hustle ginks into heaven."

Now, education is as much concerned with souls as religion is.

Religion is a Way of Life, and education is a preparation of the soul to live its life here and hereafter; to live it nobly and fully. And as we cannot think of religion without a Person as its centre, as we cannot think of a church without its Teacher, so we cannot think of a school without its Master. A school, in fact, according to the conception of our wise ancestors, was less a place than a little group of persons, a teacher and his pupils. Its place might be poor, nay, it might have no local habitation at all, it might be peripatetic: where the master went the disciples followed One may think of Our Lord and His friends as a sort of school: was He not the Master, and were not they His disciples? That gracious conception was not only the conception of the old Gael, pagan and Christian, but it was the conception of Europe all through the Middle Ages. Philosophy was not crammed out of textbooks, but was learned at the knee of some great philosopher; art was learned in the studio of some master-artist, a craft in the workshop of some master-craftsman. Always it was the personality of the master that made the school, never the State that built it of brick and mortar, drew up a code of rules to govern it, and sent hirelings into it to carry out its decrees.

I do not know how far it is possible to revive the old ideal of fosterer and foster-child. I know it were very desirable. One sees too clearly that the modern system, under which the teacher tends more and more to become a mere civil servant, is making for the degradation of education, and will end in irreligion and anarchy. The modern child is coming to regard his teacher as an official paid by the State to render him certain services; services which it is in his interest to avail of, since by doing so he will increase his earning capacity later on; but services the rendering and acceptance of which no more imply a sacred relationship than do the rendering and acceptance of the services of a dentist or a chiropodist. There is thus coming about a complete reversal of the relative positions of master and disciple, a tendency which is increased by every statute that is placed on the statute book, by every rule that is added to the education code of modern countries.

Against this trend I would oppose the ideal of those who shaped the Gaelic polity nearly two thousand years ago. It is not merely that the old Irish had a good education system; they had the best and noblest that has

ever been known among men. There has never been any human institution more adequate to its purpose than that which, in pagan times, produced Cuchulainn and the Boy-Corps of Eamhain Macha and, in Christian times, produced Enda and the companions of his solitude in Aran. The old Irish system, pagan and Christian, possessed in pre-eminent degree the thing most needful in education: an adequate inspiration. Colmcille suggested what that inspiration was when he said, "If I die it shall be from the excess of the love that I bear the Gael." A love and a service so excessive as to annihilate all thought of
self, a recognition that one must give all, must be willing always to make the ultimate sacrifice this is the inspiration alike of the story of Cuchulainn and of the story of Colmcille, the inspiration that made the one a hero and the other a saint.

VI

MASTER AND DISCIPLES

In the Middle Ages there were everywhere little groups of persons clustering round some beloved teacher, and thus it was that men learned not only the humanities but all gracious and useful crafts. There were no State art schools, no State technical schools: as I have said, men became artists in the studio of some master-artist, men learned crafts in the workshop of some master-craftsman. It was always the individual inspiring, guiding, fostering other individuals; never the State usurping the place of father or fosterer, dispensing education like a universal provider of ready-mades, aiming at turning out all men and women according to regulation patterns.

In Ireland the older and truer conception was never lost sight of. It persisted into Christian times when a Kieran or an Enda or a Colmcille gathered his little group of foster-children (the old word was still used) around him; they were collectively his family, his household, his *clann*—many sweet and endearing words were used to mark the intimacy of that relationship. It seems to me that there has been nothing nobler in the history of education than this development of the old Irish plan of fosterage under a Christian rule, when to the pagan ideals of strength and truth there were added the Christian ideals of love and humility. And this, remember, was not the education system of an aristocracy, but the education system of a people. It was more democratic than any education system in the world to-day. Our very divisions into primary, secondary, and university crystallize a snobbishness partly intellectual and partly social. At Clonard, Kieran, the son of a carpenter, sat in the same class as Colmcille, the son of a king. To Clonard or to Aran or to Clonmacnois went every man, rich or poor, prince or peasant, who wanted to sit at Finnian's or at Enda's or at Kieran's feet and to learn of his wisdom.

Always it was the personality of the teacher that drew them there. And so it was all through Irish history. A great poet or a great scholar had his foster-children who lived at his house or fared with him through the country. Even long after Kinsale the Munster poets had their little groups of pupils; and the hedge schoolmasters of the nineteenth century were the last repositories of a high tradition.

I dwell on the importance of the personal element in education. I would have every child not merely a unit in a school attendance, but in some intimate personal way the pupil of a teacher, or, to use more expressive words, the disciple of a master. And here I nowise contradict another position of mine, that the main object in education is to help the child to be his own true and best self. What the teacher should bring to his pupil is not a set of readymade opinions, or a stock of cut-and-dry information, but an inspiration and an example; and his main qualification should be, not such an overmastering will as shall impose itself at all hazards upon all weaker wills that come under its influence, but rather so infectious an enthusiasm as shall kindle new enthusiasm. The Montessori system, so admirable in many ways, would seem at first sight to attach insufficient importance to the function of the teacher in the schoolroom. But this is not really so. True, it would make the spontaneous efforts of the children the main motive power, as against the dominating will of the teacher which is the main motive power in the ordinary schoolroom. But the teacher must be there always to inspire, to foster. If you would realise how true this is, how important the personality of the teacher, even in a Montessori school, try to imagine a Montessori school conducted by the average teacher of your acquaintance, or try to imagine a Montessori school conducted by yourself!

VII

OF FREEDOM IN EDUCATION

I have claimed elsewhere that the native Irish education system possessed pre-eminently two characteristics: first, freedom for the individual, and, secondly, an adequate inspiration. Without these two things you cannot have education, no matter how you may elaborate educational machinery, no matter how you may multiply educational programmes. And because those two things are pre-eminently lacking in what passes for education in Ireland, we have in Ireland strictly no education system at all; nothing that by any extension of the meaning of words can be called an education system. We have an elaborate machinery for teaching persons certain subjects, and the teaching is done more or less efficiently; more efficiently, I imagine, than such teaching is done in England or in America. We have three universities and four boards of education. We have some thousands of buildings, large and small. We have an army of inspectors, mostly overpaid. We have a host of teachers, mostly underpaid. We have a Compulsory Education Act. We have the grave and bulky code of the Commissioners of National Education, and the slim impertinent pamphlet which enshrines the wisdom of the Commissioners of Intermediate Education. We have a vast deal more in the shape of educational machinery and stage properties. But we have, I repeat, no education system; and only in isolated places have we any education. The essentials are lacking.

And first of freedom. The word freedom is no longer understood in Ireland. We have no experience of the thing, and we have almost lost our conception of the idea. So completely is this true that the very organisations which exist in Ireland to champion freedom show no disposition themselves to accord freedom they challenge a great tyranny, but they erect their little tyrannies. "Thou shalt not" is half the law of Ireland, and the other half is "Thou must."

Now, nowhere has the law of "Thou shalt not" and "Thou must" been so rigorous as in the schoolroom. Surely the first essential of healthy life there was freedom. But there has been and there is no freedom in Irish education; no freedom for the child, no freedom for the teacher, no freedom for the school. Where young souls, young minds, young bodies, demanded the largest measure of individual freedom consistent with the common good, freedom to move and grow on their natural lines, freedom to live their own lives—for what is natural life but natural growth?—freedom to bring themselves, as I have put it elsewhere, to their own perfection, there was a sheer denial of the right of the individual to grow in his own natural way, that is, in God's way. He had to develop not in God's way, but in the Board's way. The Board, National or Intermediate as the case might be, bound him hand and foot, chained him mind and soul, constricted him morally, mentally, and physically with the involuted folds of its rules and regulations, its programmes, its minutes, its reports and special reports, its pains and penalties. I have often thought that the type of English education in Ireland was the Laocoon: that agonising father and his sons seem to me like the teacher and the pupils of an Irish school, the strong limbs of the man and the slender limbs of the boys caught together and crushed together in the grip of an awful fate. And English education in Ireland has seemed to some like the bed of Procustes, the bed on which all men that passed that way must lie, be it never so big for them, be it never so small for them: the traveller for whom it was too large had his limbs stretched until he filled it; the traveller for whom it was too small had his limbs chopped off until he fitted into it—comfortably. It was a grim jest to play upon travellers. The English have done it to Irish children not by way of jest, but with a purpose. Our English-Irish systems took, and take, absolutely no cognisance of the differences between individuals, of the differences between localities, of the differences between urban and rural communities, of the differences springing from a different ancestry,

Gaelic or Anglo-Saxon. Every school must conform to a type—and what a type! Every individual must conform to a type—and what a type! The teacher has not been at liberty, and in practice is not yet at liberty, to seek to discover the individual bents of his pupils, the hidden talent that is in every normal soul, to discover which and to cherish which, that it may in the fullness of time be put to some precious use, is the primary duty of the teacher. I knew one boy who passed through several schools a dunce and a laughing-stock; the National Board and the Intermediate Board had sat in judgment upon him and had damned him as a failure before men and angels. Yet a friend and fellow-worker of mine discovered that he was gifted with a wondrous sympathy for nature, that he loved and understood the ways of plants, that he had a strange minuteness and subtlety of observation—that, in short, he was the sort of boy likely to become an accomplished botanist. I knew another boy of whom his father said to me: "He is no good at books, he is no good at work; he is good at nothing but playing a tin whistle. What am I to do with him?" I shocked the worthy man by replying (though really it was the obvious thing to reply): "Buy a tin whistle for him." Once a colleague of mine summed up the whole philosophy of education in a maxim which startled a sober group of visitors: "If a boy shows an aptitude for doing anything better than most people, he should be encouraged to do that, and to do it as well as possible; I don't care what it is—scotch-hop, if you like."

The idea of a compulsory programme imposed by an external authority upon every child in every school in a country is the direct contrary of the root idea involved in education. Yet this is what we have in Ireland. In theory the primary schools have a certain amount of freedom; in practice they have none. Neither in theory nor in practice is such a thing as freedom dreamt of in the gloomy limbo whose presiding demon is the Board of Intermediate Education for Ireland. Education, indeed, reaches its nadir in the Irish Intermediate system. At the present moment there are 15,000 boys and girls pounding at a programme drawn up for them by certain persons sitting round a table in Hume Street. Precisely the same textbooks are being read to-night in every secondary school and college in Ireland. Two of Hawthorne's Tanglewood Tales, with a few poems in English, will constitute the whole literary pabulum of three-quarters of the pupils of the Irish secondary schools during this twelvemonths.[2] The teacher who seeks to give his pupils a wider horizon in literature does so at his peril. He will, no doubt, benefit his pupils, but he will infallibly reduce his results fees. As an intermediate teacher said to me, "Culture is all very well in its way, but if you don't stick to your programme your boys won't pass." "Stick to your programme" is the strange device on the banner of the Irish Intermediate system; and the programme bulks so large that there is no room for education.

The first thing I plead for, therefore, is freedom: freedom for each school to shape its own programme in conformity with the circumstances of the school as to place, size, personnel, and so on; freedom again for the individual teacher to impart something of his own personality to his work, to bring his own peculiar gifts to the service of his pupils, to be, in short, a teacher, a master, one having an intimate and permanent relationship with his pupils, and not a mere part of the educational machine, a mere cog in the wheel; freedom finally for the individual pupil and scope for his development within the school and within the system. And I would promote this idea of freedom by the very organisation of the school itself, giving a certain autonomy not only to the school, but to the particular parts of the school: to the staff, of course, but also to the pupils, and, in a large school, to the various subdivisions of the pupils. I do not plead for anarchy. I plead for freedom within the law, for liberty, not license, for that true freedom which can exist only where there is discipline, which exists in fact because each, valuing his own freedom, respects also the freedom of others.

---

[2] 1912-13

VIII

BACK TO THE SAGAS

That freedom may be availed of to the noble ends of education there must be, within the school system and within the school, an adequate inspiration. The school must make such an appeal to the pupil as shall resound throughout his after life, urging him always to be his best self, never his second-best self. Such an inspiration will come most adequately of all from religion. I do not think that there can be any education of which spiritual religion does not form an integral part; as it is the most important part of life, so it should be the most important part of education, which some have defined as a preparation for complete life. And inspiration will come also from the hero-stories of the world, and especially of our own people; from science and art if taught by people who are really scientists and artists, and not merely persons with certificates from Mr. T. W. Russell; from literature enjoyed as literature and not studied as "texts;" from the associations of the school place; finally and chiefly from the humanity and great-heartedness of the teacher.

A heroic tale is more essentially a factor in education than a proposition in Euclid. The story of Joan of Arc or the story of the young Napoleon means more for boys and girls than all the algebra in all the books. What the modern world wants more than anything else, what Ireland wants beyond all other modern countries, is a new birth of the heroic spirit. If our schools would set themselves that task, the task of fostering once again knightly courage and strength and truth —that type of efficiency rather than the peculiar type of efficiency demanded by the English Civil Service—we should have at least the beginning of an educational system. And what an appeal an Irish school system might have! What a rallying cry an Irish Minister of Education might give to young Ireland! When we were starting St. Enda's I said to my boys: "We must re-create and perpetuate in Ireland the knightly tradition of Cuchulainn, 'better is short life with honour than long life with dishonour;' 'I care not though I were to live but one day and one night, if only my fame and my deeds live after me;' the noble tradition of the Fianna, 'we, the Fianna, never told a lie, falsehood was never imputed to us;' 'strength in our hands, truth on our lips, and cleanness in our hearts;' the Christ-like tradition of Colmcille, 'if I die it shall be from the excess of the love I bear the Gael." And to that antique evangel should be added the evangels of later days: the stories of Red Hugh and Wolfe Tone and Robert Emmet and John Mitchel and O'Donovan Rossa and Eoghan O'Growney. I have seen Irish boys and girls moved inexpressibly by the story of Emmet or the story of Anne Devlin, and I have always felt it to be legitimate to make use for educational purposes of an exaltation so produced.

The value of the national factor in education would appear to rest chiefly in this, that it addresses itself to the most generous side of the child's nature, urging him to live up to his finest self. If the true work of the teacher be, as I have said, to help the child to realise himself at his best and worthiest, the factor of nationality is of prime importance, apart from any ulterior propagandist views the teacher may cherish. The school system which neglects it commits, even from the purely pedagogic point of view, a primary blunder. It neglects one of the most powerful of educational resources.

It is because the English education system in Ireland has deliberately eliminated the national factor that it has so terrifically succeeded. For it has succeeded—succeeded in making slaves of us. And it has succeeded so well that we no longer realise that we are slaves. Some of us even think our chains ornamental, and are a little doubtful as to whether we shall be quite as comfortable and quite as respectable when they are hacked off.

It remains the crowning achievement of the "National" and Intermediate systems that they have wrought such a change in this people that once loved freedom so passionately. Three-quarters of a century ago there still remained in Ireland a stubborn Irish thing which Cromwell had not trampled out, which the Penal Laws had not crushed, which the horrors of '98 had not daunted, which Pitt had not purchased: a national consciousness enshrined mainly in a national language. After three-quarters of a century's education that thing is nearly lost.

A new education system in Ireland has to do more than restore a national culture. It has to restore manhood to a race that has been deprived of it. Along with its inspiration it must, therefore, bring a certain hardening. It must lead Ireland back to her sagas.

Finally, I say, inspiration must come from the teacher. If we can no longer send the children to the heroes and seers and scholars to be fostered, we can at least bring some of the heroes and seers and scholars to the schools. We can rise up against the system which tolerates as teachers the rejected of all other professions rather than demanding for so priest-like an office the highest souls and noblest intellects of the race. I remember once going into a schoolroom in Belgium and finding an old man talking quietly and beautifully about literature to a silent class of boys; I was told that he was one of the most distinguished of contemporary Flemish poets. Here was the sort of personality, the sort of influence, one ought to see in a schoolroom. Not, indeed, that every poet would make a good schoolmaster, or every schoolmaster a good poet. But how seldom here has the teacher any interest in literature at all; how seldom has he any horizon above his timetable, any soul larger than his results fees!

The fact is that, with rare exceptions, the men and women who are willing to work under the conditions as to personal dignity, freedom, tenure, and emolument which obtain in Irish schools are not the sort of men and women likely to make good educators. This part of the subject has been so much discussed in public that one need not dwell upon it. We are all alive to the truth that a teacher ought to be paid better than a policeman, and to the scandal of the fact that many an able and cultured man is working in Irish secondary schools at a salary less than that of the Viceroy's chauffeur.

IX

WHEN WE ARE FREE

In these chapters I have sufficiently indicated the general spirit in which I would have Irish education re-created. I say little of organisation, of mere machinery. That is the least important part of the subject. We can all foresee that the first task of a free Ireland must be destructive: that the lusty strokes of Gael and Gall, Ulster taking its manful part, will hew away and cast adrift the rotten and worm-eaten boards which support the grotesque fabric of the English education system. We can all see that, when in Irish Government is constituted, there will be an Irish Minister of Education responsible to the Irish Parliament; that under him Irish education will be drawn into a homogeneous whole—an organic unity will replace composite freak in which the various members are not only not directed by a single intelligence but are often mutually antagonistic, and sometimes engaged in open warfare one with the other, like the preposterous donkey in the pantomime whose head is in perpetual strife with his heels because they belong to different individuals. The individual entities that compose the English-Irish educational donkey are four: the Commissioners of National Education, the Commissioners of Intermediate Education, the Commissioners of Education for certain Endowed Schools, and last, but not least, the Department of Agriculture and Technical Instruction—the modern Ioldanach which in this realm protects science, art, fishery, needlework, poultry, foods and drugs, horse-breeding, etc., etc., etc., etc., and whose versatile chiefs can at a moment's notice switch off their attention from archaeology in the Nile Valley to the Foot and Mouth Disease in Mullingar. I must admit that the educational work of the Department as far as it affects secondary schools is done efficiently; but one will naturally expect this branch of its activity to be brought into the general education scheme under the Minister of Education. In addition to the four Boards I have enumerated I need hardly say that Dublin Castle has its finger in the pie, as it has in every unsavoury pie in Ireland. And behind Dublin Castle looms the master of Dublin Castle, and the master of all the Boards, and the master of everything in Ireland—the British Treasury—arrogating claims over the veriest details of education in Ireland for which there is no parallel in any other administration in the world and no sanction even in the British Constitution. My scheme, of course, presupposes the getting rid not only of the British Treasury, but of the British connection.

One perceives the need, too, of linking up the whole system and giving it a common impulse. Under the Minister there might well be chiefs of the various subdivisions, elementary, secondary, higher, and technical; but these should not be independent potentates, each entrenched in a different stronghold in a different part of the city. I do not see why they could not all occupy offices in the same corridor of the same building. The whole government of the free kingdom of Belgium was carried on in one small building. A Council of some sort, with subcommittees, would doubtless be associated with the Minister, but I think its function should be advisory rather than executive: that all acts should be the acts of the Minister. As to the local organisation of elementary schools, there will always be need of a local manager, and personally I see no reason why the local management should be given to a district council rather than left as it is at present to some individual in the locality interested in education, but a thousand reasons why it should not. I would, however, make the teachers, both primary and secondary, a national service, guaranteeing an adequate salary, adequate security of tenure, adequate promotion, and adequate pension: and all this means adequate endowment, and freedom from the control of parsimonious officials.

In the matter of language, I would order things bilingually. But I would not apply the Belgian system exactly as I have described it in *An Claidheamh Soluis*[3]. The *status quo* in Ireland is different from that in Belgium; the ideal to be aimed at in Ireland is different from that in Belgium. Ireland is six-sevenths English-speaking with an Irish-

---

[3] Irish nationalist newspaper whose title translates to "Sword of Light." In publication from 1899-1931, it was edited by Pearse from 1903-1909.

speaking seventh. Belgium is divided into two nearly equal halves, one Flemish, the other French. Irish Nationalists would restore Irish as a vernacular to the English-speaking six-sevenths, and would establish Irish as the national language of a free Ireland: Belgian Nationalists would simply preserve their "two national languages," according them equal rights and privileges. What then? Irish should be made the language of instruction in districts where it is the home language, and English the "second language," taught as a school subject: I would not at any stage use English as a medium of instruction in such districts, anything that I have elsewhere said as to Belgian practice notwithstanding. Where English is the home language it must of necessity be the "first language" in the schools, but I would have a compulsory "second language," satisfied that this "second language" in five-sixths of the schools would be Irish. And I would see that the "second language" be utilised as a medium of instruction from the earliest stages. In this way, and in no other way that I can imagine, can Irish be restored as a vernacular to English-speaking Ireland.

But in all the details of their programmes the schools should have autonomy. The function of the central authority should be to coordinate, to maintain a standard, to advise, to inspire, to keep the teachers in touch with educational thought in other lands. I would transfer the centre of gravity of the system from the education office to the teachers; the teachers in fact would be the system. Teachers, and not clerks, would henceforth conduct the education of the country.

The inspectors, again, would be selected from the teachers, and the chiefs of departments from the inspectors. And promoted teachers would man the staffs of the training colleges, which, for the rest, would work in close touch with the universities.

I need hardly say that the present Intermediate system must be abolished. Good men will curse it in its passing. It is the most evil thing that Ireland has ever known. Dr. Hyde once finely described the National and Intermediate Boards as:

"Death and the nightmare Death-in-Life
That thicks men's blood with cold."

Of the two Death-in-Life is the more hideous. It is sleeker than, but equally as obscene as, its fellow-fiend. The thing has damned more souls than the Drink Traffic or the White Slave Traffic. Down with it down among the dead men I Let it promote competitive examinations in the underworld, if it will.

Well-trained and well-paid teachers, well-equipped and beautiful schools, and a fund at the disposal of each school to enable it to award prizes on its own tests based on its own programme—these would be among the characteristics of a new secondary system. Manual work, both indoor and outdoor, would, I hope, be part of the programme of every school. And the internal organisation might well follow the models of the little child-republics I have elsewhere described, with their own laws and leaders, their fostering of individualities yet never at the expense of the common wealth, their care for the body as well as for the mind, their nobly-ordered games, their spacious outdoor life, their intercourse with the wild things of the woods and wastes, their daily adventure face to face with elemental Life and Force, with its moral discipline, with its physical hardening.

And then, vivifying the whole, we need the divine breath that moves through free peoples, the breath that no man of Ireland has felt in his nostrils for so many centuries, the breath that once blew through the streets of Athens and that kindled, as wine kindles, the hearts of those who taught and learned in Clonmacnoise[4].

---

[4] Irish Catholic Monastery and Cathedral established in AD 544 and disestablished in 1568. The ruins of the site are revered to this day.

HOW DOES SHE STAND?

THREE ADDRESSES

I

THEOBALD WOLFE TONE[5]

We have come to the holiest place in Ireland; holier to us even than the place where Patrick sleeps in Down. Patrick brought us life, but this man died for us. And though many before him and some since have died in testimony of the truth of Ireland's claim to nationhood, Wolfe Tone was the greatest of all that have made that testimony, the greatest of all that have died for Ireland whether in old time or in new. He was the greatest of Irish Nationalists; I believe he was the greatest of Irish men. And if I am right in this I am right in saying that we stand in the holiest place in Ireland, for it must be that the holiest sod of a nation's soil is the sod where the greatest of her dead lies buried.

I feel it difficult to speak to you to-day; difficult to speak in this place. It is as if one had to speak by the graveside of some dear friend, a brother in blood or a well-tried comrade in arms, and to say aloud the things one would rather keep to oneself. But I am helped by the knowledge that you who listen to me partake in my emotion: we are none of us strangers, being all in a sense own brothers to Tone, sharing in his faith, sharing in his hope, still unrealised, sharing in his great love. I

---

[5] An Address delivered at the Grave of Wolfe Tone in Bodenstown Churchyard, 22nd June, 1913.

have, then, only to find expression for the thoughts and emotions common to us all, and you will understand even if the expression be a halting one.

We have come here not merely to salute this noble dust and to pay our homage to the noble spirit of Tone. We have come to renew our adhesion to the faith of Tone; to express once more our full acceptance of the gospel of Irish Nationalism which he was the first to formulate in worthy terms, giving clear definition and plenary meaning to all that had been thought and taught before him by Irish-speaking and English-speaking men; uttered half articulately by a Shane O'Neill in some defiance flung at the Englishry, expressed under some passionate metaphor by a Geoffrey Keating, hinted at by a Swift in some biting gibe, but clearly and greatly stated by Wolfe Tone, and not needing now ever to be stated anew for any new generation. He has spoken for all time, and his voice resounds throughout Ireland, calling to us from this grave when we wander astray following other voices that ring less true.

This, then, is the first part of Wolfe Tone's achievement he made articulate the dumb voices of the centuries, he gave Ireland a clear and precise and worthy concept of Nationality. But he did more than this: not only did he define Irish Nationalism, but he armed his generation in defence of it. Thinker and doer, dreamer of the immortal dream and doer of the immortal deed—we owe to this dead man more than we can ever repay him by making pilgrimages to his grave or by rearing to him the stateliest monument in the streets of his city. To his teaching we owe it that there is such a thing as Irish Nationalism, and to the memory of the deed he nerved his generation to do, to the memory of '98, we owe it that there is any manhood left in Ireland.

I have called him the greatest of our dead. In mind he was great above all the men of his time or of the after time; and he was greater still in spirit. It was to that nobly-dowered mind of his that Kickham, himself the most nobly-dowered of a later generation, paid reverence when he said:

> "Oh, knowledge is a wondrous power;
> 'Tis stronger than the wind.

And would to the kind heavens
That Wolfe Tone were here to-day."

But greater than that full-orbed intelligence, that wide, gracious, richly stored mind, was the mighty spirit of Tone. This man's soul was a burning flame, a flame so ardent, so generous, so pure, that to come into communion with it is to come unto a new baptism, unto a new regeneration and cleansing. If we who stand by this graveside could make ourselves at one with the heroic spirit that once inbreathed this clay, could in some way come into loving contact with it, possessing ourselves of something of its ardour, its valour, its purity, its tenderness, its gaiety, how good a thing it would be for us, how good a thing for Ireland; with what joyousness and strength should we set our faces towards the path that lies before us, bringing with us fresh life from this place of death, a new resurrection of patriotic grace in our souls!

Try to get near the spirit of Tone, the gallant soldier spirit, the spirit that dared and soared, the spirit that loved and served, the spirit that laughed and sang with the gladness of a boy. I do not ask you to venerate him as a saint; I ask you to love him as a man. For myself, I would rather have known this man than any man of whom I have ever heard or ever read. I have not read or heard of any had more of heroic stuff in him than he, any that went so gaily and so gallantly about a great deed, any who loved so well, any who was so beloved. To have been this man's friend, what a privilege that would have been! To have known him as Thomas Russell knew him! I have always loved the very name of Thomas Russell because Tone so loved him.

I do not think there has ever been a more true and loyal man than Tone. He had for his friends an immense tenderness and charity; and now and then there breaks into what he is writing or saying a gust of passionate love for his wife, for his children. "O my babies, my babies!" he exclaims... Yes, this man could love well; and it was from such love as this he exiled himself; with such love as this crushed in his faithful heart that he became a weary but indomitable ambassador to courts and camps; with the memory of such love as this, with the little hands of his children plucking at his heart-strings, that he lay down to die in that cell on Arbour Hill.

Such is the high and sorrowful destiny of the heroes: to turn their backs to the pleasant paths and their faces to the hard paths, to blind their eyes to the fair things of life, to stifle all sweet music in the heart, the low voices of women and the laughter of little children, and to follow only the far, faint call that leads them into the battle or to the harder death at the foot of a gibbet.

Think of Tone. Think of his boyhood and young manhood in Dublin and Kildare, his adventurous spirit and plans, his early love and marriage, his glorious failure at the bar, his healthy contempt for what he called "a foolish wig and gown," and then—the call of Ireland. Think of how he put virility into the Catholic movement, how this heretic toiled to make free men of Catholic helots, how, as he worked among them, he grew to know and to love the real, the historic Irish people, and the great, clear, sane conception came to him that in Ireland there must be, not two nations or three nations, but one nation, that Protestant and Dissenter must be brought into amity with Catholic, and that Catholic, Protestant, and Dissenter must unite to achieve freedom for all.

Then came the United Irishmen, and those journeys through Ireland—to Ulster and to Connacht—which, as described by him, read like epics infused with a kindly human humour. Soon the Government realises that this is the most dangerous man in Ireland—this man who preaches peace among brother Irishmen. It does not suit the Government that peace and goodwill between Catholic and Protestant should be preached in Ireland. So Tone goes into exile, having first pledged himself to the cause of Irish freedom on the Cave Hill above Belfast. From America to France: one of the great implacable exiles of Irish history, a second and a greater Fitzmaurice, one might say to him as the poet said to Sarsfield:

"Ag déanamh do ghearáin leis na ríghthibh Is gur fhág tú Eire 's Gaedhil bhocht' claoidhte,

Och, ochón!"

30

But it was no "complaint" that Tone made to foreign rulers and foreign senates, but wise and bold counsel that he gave them; wise because bold. A French fleet ploughs the waves and enters Bantry Bay— Tone on board. We know the sequel: how the fleet tossed about for days on the broad bosom of the Bay, how the craven in command refused to make a landing because his commander-in-chief had not come up, how Tone's heart was torn with impatience and yearning—he saw his beloved Ireland, could see the houses and the people on shore—how the fleet set sail, that deed undone that would have freed Ireland.

It is the supreme tribute to the greatness of this man that after that cruel disappointment he set to work again, indomitable. Two more expeditions, a French and a Dutch, were fitted out for Ireland, but never reached Ireland. Then at last came Tone himself; he had said he would come, if need be, with only a corporal's guard: he came with very little more.

Three small ships enter Lough Swilly The English follow them. Tone's vessel fights: Tone commands one of the guns. For six hours she stood alone against the whole English fleet. What a glorious six hours for Tone! A battered hulk, the vessel struck; Tone, betrayed by a friend, was dragged to Dublin and condemned to a traitor's death. Then the last scene in the Provost Prison, and Tone lies dead, the greatest of the men of '98. To this spot they bore him, and here he awaits the judgment; and we stand at his graveside and remember that his work is still unaccomplished after more than a hundred years.

When men come to a graveside they pray; and each of us prays here in his heart. But we do not pray for Tone—men who die that their people may be free "have no need of prayer." We pray for Ireland that she may be free, and for ourselves that we may free her. My brothers, were it not an unspeakable privilege if to our generation it should be granted to accomplish that which Tone's generation, so much worthier than ours, failed to accomplish! To complete the work of Tone!....

And let us make no mistake as to what Tone sought to do, what it remains for us to do. We need not re-state our programme; Tone has stated it for us:

"To break the connection with England, the never-failing source of all our political evils, and to assert the independence of my country these were my objects. To unite the whole people of Ireland, to abolish the memory of all past dissensions, and to substitute the common name of Irishmen in place of the denominations of Protestant, Catholic, and Dissenter—these were my means."

I find here implicit all the philosophy of Irish Nationalism, all the teaching of the Gaelic League and the later prophets. Ireland one and Ireland free—is not this the definition of Ireland a Nation? To that definition and to that programme we declare our adhesion anew; pledging ourselves as Tone pledged himself—and in this sacred place, by this graveside, let us not pledge ourselves unless we mean to keep our pledge—we pledge ourselves to follow in the steps of Tone, never to rest, either by day or by night, until his work be accomplished, deeming it the proudest of all privileges to fight for freedom, to fight, not in despondency, but in great joy, hoping for the victory in our day, but fighting on whether victory seem near or far, never lowering our ideal, never bartering one jot or tittle of our birth-right, holding faith to the memory and the inspiration of Tone, and accounting ourselves base as long as we endure the evil thing against which he testified with his blood.

II

ROBERT EMMET AND THE IRELAND
OF TO-DAY

I[6]

You ask me to speak of the Ireland of to-day. What can I tell you of
it that is worthy of commemoration where we commemorate heroic faith
and the splendour of death? In that Ireland whose spokesmen have, in
return for the promise of a poor simulacrum of liberty, pledged to our
ancient enemy our loyalty and the loyalty of our children, is there, even
though that pledge has been spoken, any group of true men, any right
striving, any hope still cherished in virtue of which, lifting up our hearts,
we can cry across the years to him whom we remember to-night,
"Brother, we have kept the faith; comrade, we, too, stand ready to
serve?"

For patriotism is at once a faith and a service. A faith which in some
of us has been in our flesh and bone since we were moulded in our
mothers' wombs, and which in others of us has at some definite moment
of our later lives been kindled flaming as if by the miraculous word of
God; a faith which is of the same nature as religious faith and is one of
the eternal witnesses in the heart of man to the truth that we are of divine
kindred; a faith which, like religious faith, when true and vital, is
wonder-working, but, like religious faith, is dead without good works
even as the body without the spirit. So that patriotism needs service as
the condition of its authenticity, and it is not sufficient to say "I believe"
unless one can say also "I serve."

And our patriotism is measured, not by the formula in which we

---

[6] An Address delivered at the Emmet Commemoration in the Academy of
Music, Brooklyn, New York, 2nd March, 1914.

33

declare it, but by the service which we render. We owe to our country all fealty and she asks always for our service; and there are times when she asks of us not ordinary but some supreme service. There are in every generation those who shrink from the ultimate sacrifice, but there are in every generation those who make it with joy and laughter, and these are the salt of the generations, the heroes who stand midway between God and men. Patriotism is in large part a memory of heroic dead men and a striving to accomplish some task left unfinished by them. Had they not gone before, made their attempts and suffered the sorrow of their failures, we should long ago have lost the tradition of faith and service, having no memory in the heart nor any unaccomplished dream.

The generation that is now growing old in Ireland had almost forgotten our heroes. We had learned the great art of parleying with our enemy and achieving nationhood by negotiation. The heroes had trodden hard and bloody ways: we should tread soft and flowering ways. The heroes had given up all things: we had learned a way of gaining all things, land and good living and the friendship of our foe. But the soil of Ireland, yea, the very stones of our cities have cried out against an infidelity that would barter an old tradition of nationhood even for a thing so precious as peace. This the heroes have done for us; for their spirits indwell in the place where they lived, and the hills of Ireland must be rent and her cities levelled with the ground and all her children driven out upon the seas of the world before those voices are silenced that bid us be faithful still and to make no peace with England until Ireland is ours.

I live in a place that is very full of heroic memories. In the room in which I work at St. Enda's College, Robert Emmet is said often to have sat; in our garden is a vine which they call Emmet's Vine and from which he is said to have plucked grapes; through our wood runs a path which is called Emmet's Walk—they say that he and Sarah Curran walked there; at an angle of our boundary wall there is a little fortified lodge called Emmet's Fort. Across the road from us is a thatched cottage whose tenant in 1803 was in Green Street Courthouse all the long day that Emmet stood on trial, with a horse saddled without that he might bring news of the end to Sarah Curran. Half a mile from us across the fields is

Butterfield House, where Emmet lived during the days preceding the rising. It is easy to imagine his figure coming out along the Harold's Cross Road to Rathfarnham, tapping the ground with his cane, as they say was his habit; a young, slight figure, with how noble a head bent a little upon the breast, with how high a heroism sleeping underneath that quietness and gravity! One thinks of his anxious nights in Butterfield House; of his busy days in Marshalsea Lane or Patrick Street; of his careful plans—the best plans that have yet been made for the capture of Dublin; his inventions and devices, the jointed pikes, the rockets and explosives upon which he counted so much; his ceaseless conferences, his troubles with his associates, his disappointments, his disillusionments, borne with such sweetness and serenity of temper, such a trust in human nature, such a trust in Ireland! Then the hurried rising, the sally into the streets, the failure at the Castle gates, the catastrophe in Thomas Street, the retreat along the familiar Harold's Cross Road to Rathfarnham. At Butterfield House Anne Devlin, the faithful, keeps watch. You remember her greeting to Emmet in the first pain of her disappointment: "Musha, bad welcome to you! Is Ireland lost by you, cowards that you are, to lead the people to destruction and then to leave them?" And poor Emmet's reply—no word of blame for the traitors that had sold him, for the cravens that had abandoned him, for the fools that had bungled; just a halting, heartbroken exculpation, the only one he was to make for himself—"Don't blame me, Anne; the fault is not mine." And her woman's heart went out to him and she took him in and cherished him; but the soldiery were on his track, and that was his last night in Butterfield House. The bracken was his bed thenceforth, or a precarious pillow in his old quarters at Harold's Cross, until he lay down in Kilmainham to await the summons of the executioner.

No failure, judged as the world judges these things, was ever more complete, more pathetic than Emmet's. And yet he has left us a prouder memory than the memory of Brian victorious at Clontarf or of Owen Roe victorious at Benburb. It is the memory of a sacrifice Christ-like in its perfection. Dowered with all things splendid and sweet, he left all things and elected to die. Face to face with England in the dock at Green Street he uttered the most memorable words ever uttered by an Irish man: words which, ringing clear above a century's tumults, forbid us ever to waver or grow weary until our country takes her place among the nations of the earth. And his death was august. In the great space of Thomas Street an immense silent crowd; in front of Saint Catherine's Church a gallows upon a platform; a young man climbs to it, quiet, serene, almost smiling, they say—ah, he was very brave; there is no cheer from the crowd, no groan; this man is to die for them, but no man dares to say aloud "God bless you, Robert Emmet." Dublin must one day wash out in blood the shameful memory of that quiescence. Would Michael Dwyer come from the Wicklow Hills? Up to the last moment Emmet seems to have expected him. He was saying "Not yet" when the hangman kicked aside the plank and his body was launched into the air. They say it swung for half-an-hour, with terrible contortions, before he died. When he was dead the comely head was severed from the body. A friend of mine knew an old woman who told him how the blood flowed down upon the pavement, and how she sickened with horror as she saw the dogs of the street lap up that noble blood. Then the hangman showed the pale head to the people and announced: "This is the head of a traitor, Robert Emmet." A traitor? No, but a true man. O my brothers, this was one of the truest men that ever lived. This was one of the bravest spirits that Ireland has ever nurtured. This man was faithful even unto the ignominy of the gallows, dying that his people might live, even as Christ died.

Be assured that such a death always means a redemption. Emmet redeemed Ireland from acquiescence in the Union. His attempt was not a failure, but a triumph for that deathless thing we call Irish Nationality. It was by Emmet that men remembered Ireland until Davis and Mitchel took up his work again, and '48 handed on the tradition to '67, and from '67 we receive the tradition unbroken.

You ask me to speak of the Ireland of to-day. What need I say but that to-day Ireland is turning her face once more to the old path? Nothing seems more definitely to emerge when one looks at the movements that are stirring both above the surface and beneath the surface in men's minds at home than the fact that the new generation is reaffirming the Fenian faith, the faith of Emmet. It is because we know that this is so that we can suffer in patience the things that are said and done in the name of Irish Nationality by some of our leaders. What one may call the Westminster phase is passing: the National movement is swinging back again into its proper channel. A new junction has been made with the past: into the movement that has never wholly died since '67 have come the young men of the Gaelic League. Having renewed communion with its origins, Irish Nationalism is to-day a more virile thing than ever before in our time. Of that be sure.

I have said again and again that when the Gaelic League was founded in 1893 the Irish Revolution began. The Gaelic League brought it a certain distance upon its way; but the Gaelic League could not accomplish the Revolution. For five or six years a new phase has been due, and lo! it is with us now. To-day Ireland is once more organising, once more learning the noble trade of arms. In our towns and country places Volunteer companies are springing up. Dublin pointed the way, Galway has followed Dublin, Cork has followed Galway, Wexford has followed Cork, Limerick has followed Wexford, Monaghan has followed Limerick, Sligo has followed Monaghan, Donegal has followed Sligo. There is again in Ireland the murmur of a marching, and talk of guns and tactics. What this movement may mean for our country no man can say. But it is plain to all that the existence on Irish soil of an Irish army is the most portentous fact that has appeared in Ireland for over a hundred years: a fact which marks definitely the beginning of the second stage of the Revolution which was commenced when the Gaelic League was founded. The inner significance of the movement lies in this, that men of every rank and class, of every section of Nationalist opinion, of every shade of religious belief, have discovered that they share a common patriotism, that their faith is one and that there is one service in which they can come together at last: the service of their country in arms. We are realising now how proud a thing it is to serve, and in the comradeship and joy of the new service we are forgetting many ancient misunderstandings. In the light of a rediscovered citizenship things are plain to us that were before obscure:

"Lo, a clearness of vision has followed, lo, a purification
    of sight;

Lo, the friend is discerned from the foeman, the wrong
recognised from the right."

After all, there are in Ireland but two parties: those who stand for the
English connection and those who stand against it. On what side, think
you, stand the Irish Volunteers? I cannot speak for the Volunteers; I am
not authorised to say when they will use their arms or where or how. I
can speak only for myself; and it is strictly a personal perception that I
am recording, but a perception that to me is very clear, when I say that
before this generation has passed the Volunteers will draw the sword of
Ireland. There is no truth but the old truth and no way but the old way.
Home Rule may come or may not come, but under Home Rule or in its
absence there remains for the Volunteers and for Ireland the substantial
business or achieving Irish nationhood. And I do not know how
nationhood is achieved except by armed men; I do not know how
nationhood is guarded except by armed men.

I ask you, then, to salute with me the Irish Volunteers. I ask you to
mark their advent as an augury that, no matter what pledges may be given
by men who do not know Ireland—the stubborn soul of Ireland—that
nation of ancient faith will never sell her birthright of freedom for a mess
of pottage; a mess of dubious pottage, at that. Ireland has been guilty of
many meannesses, of many shrinkings back when she should have
marched forward; but she will never be guilty of that immense infidelity.

III

ROBERT EMMET AND THE IRELAND OF TO-DAY

II[7]

We who speak here to-night are the voice of one of the ancient indestructible things of the world. We are the voice of an idea which is older than any empire and will outlast every empire. We and ours, the inheritors of that idea, have been at age-long war with one of the most powerful empires that have ever been built up upon the earth; and that empire will pass before we pass. We are older than England and we are stronger than England. In every generation we have renewed the struggle, and so it shall be unto the end. When England thinks she has trampled out our battle in blood, some brave man rises and rallies us again; when England thinks she has purchased us with a bribe, some good man redeems us by a sacrifice. Wherever England goes on her mission of empire we meet her and we strike at her; yesterday it was on the South African veldt, to-day it is in the Senate House at Washington, to-morrow it may be in the streets of Dublin. We pursue her like a sleuth-hound; we lie in wait for her and come upon her like a thief in the night; and some day we will overwhelm her with the wrath of God.

It is not that we are apostles of hate. Who like us has carried Christ's word of charity about the earth? But the Christ that said "My peace I leave you, My peace I give you," is the same Christ that said "I bring not peace, but a sword." There can be no peace between right and wrong, between truth and falsehood, between justice and oppression, between

---

[7] An Address delivered at the Emmet Commemoration in the Aeolian Hall, New York, 9th March, 1914.

freedom and tyranny. Between them it is eternal war until the wrong is righted, until the true thing is established, until justice is accomplished, until freedom is won.

So when England talks of peace we know our answer: "Peace with you? Peace while your one hand is at our throat and your other hand is in our pocket? Peace with a footpad? Peace with a pickpocket? Peace with the leech that is sucking our body dry of blood? Peace with the many-armed monster whose tentacles envelop us while its system emits an inky fluid that shrouds its work of murder from the eyes of men? The time has not yet come to talk of peace."

But England, we are told, offers us terms. She holds out to us the hand of friendship. She gives us a Parliament with an Executive responsible to it. Within two years the Home Rule Senate meets in College Green and King George comes to Dublin to declare its sessions open. In anticipation of that happy event our leaders have proffered England our loyalty. Mr. Redmond accepts Home Rule as a "final settlement between the two nations;" Mr. O'Brien in the fulness of his heart cries "God Save the King;" Colonel Lynch offers England his sword in case she is attacked by a foreign power.

And so this settlement is to be a final settlement. Would Wolfe Tone have accepted it as a final settlement? Would Robert Emmet have accepted it as a final settlement? Either we are heirs to their principles or we are not. If we are, we can accept no settlement as final which does not "*break the connection with England, the never-failing source of all our political evils*;" if we are not, how dare we go in annual pilgrimage to Bodenstown, how dare we gather here or anywhere to commemorate the faith and sacrifice of Emmet? Did, then, these dead heroic men live in vain? Has Ireland learned a truer philosophy than the philosophy of '98, and a nobler way of salvation than the way of 1803? Is Wolfe Tone's definition superseded, and do we discharge our duty to Emmet's memory by according him annually our pity?

To do the English justice, I do not think they are satisfied that Ireland will accept Home Rule as a final settlement. I think they are a little anxious to-day. If their minds were tranquil on the subject of Irish loyalty they would hardly have proclaimed the importation of arms into

Ireland the moment the Irish Volunteers had begun to organise themselves. They had given the Ulster faction which is used as a catspaw by one of the English parties two years to organise and arm against that Home Rule Bill which they profess themselves so anxious to pass: to the Nationalists of Ireland they did not give two weeks. Of course, we can arm in spite of them: to-day we are organising and training the men and we have ways and means of getting arms when the men are ready for the arms. The contention I make now, and I ask you to note it well, is that England does not trust Ireland with guns; that under Home Rule or in the absence of Home Rule England declares that we Irish must remain an unarmed people; and England is right.

England is right in suspecting Irish loyalty, and those Irishmen who promise Irish loyalty to England are wrong. I believe them honest; but they have spent so much of their lives parleying with the English, they have sat so often and so long at English feasts, that they have lost communion with the ancient unpurchaseable faith of Ireland, the ancient stubborn thing that forbids, as if with the voice of fate, any loyalty from Ireland to England, any union between us and them, any surrender of one jot or shred of our claim to freedom even in return for all the blessings of the British peace.

I have called that old faith an indestructible thing. I have said that it is more powerful than empires. If you would understand its might you must consider how it has made all the generations of Ireland heroic. Having its root in all gentleness, in a man's love for the place where his mother bore him, for the breast that gave him suck, for the voices of children that sounded in a house now silent, for the faces that glowed around a fireside now cold, for the story told by lips that will not speak again, having its root, I say, in all gentleness, it is yet a terrible thing urging the generations to perilous bloody attempts, nerving men to give up life for the death-in-life of dungeons, teaching little boys to die with laughing lips, giving courage to young girls to bare their backs to the lashes of a soldiery.

It is easy to imagine how the spirit of Irish patriotism called to the gallant and adventurous spirit of Tone or moved the wrathful spirit of Mitchel. In them deep called unto deep: heroic effort claimed the heroic

41

man. But consider how the call was made to a spirit of different, yet not less noble mould; and how it was answered. In Emmet it called to a dreamer and he awoke a man of action; it called to a student and a recluse and he stood forth a leader of men; it called to one who loved the ways of peace and he became a revolutionary. I wish I could help you to realise, I wish I could myself adequately realise, the humanity, the gentle and grave humanity, of Emmet. We are so dominated by the memory of that splendid death of his, by the memory of that young figure, serene and smiling, climbing to the gallows above that sea of silent men in Thomas Street, that we forget the life of which that death was only the necessary completion; and the life has a nearer meaning for us than the death. For Emmet, finely gifted though he was, was just a young man with the same limitations, the same self-questionings, the same falterings, the same kindly human emotions surging up sometimes in such strength as almost to drown a heroic purpose, as many a young man we have known. And his task was just such a task as many of us have undertaken: he had to go through the same repellant routine of work, to deal with the hard, uncongenial details of correspondence and committee meetings; he had the same sordid difficulties that we have, yea, even the vulgar difficulty of want of funds. And he had the same poor human material to work with, men who misunderstood, men who bungled, men who talked too much, men who failed at the last moment....

Yes, the task we take up again is just Emmet's task of silent unattractive work, the routine of correspondence and committees and organising. We must face it as bravely and as quietly as he faced it, working on in patience as he worked on, hoping as he hoped; cherishing in our secret hearts the mighty hope that to us, though so unworthy, it may be given to bring to accomplishment the thing he left unaccomplished, but working on even when that hope dies within us.

I would ask you to consider now how the call I have spoken of was made to the spirit of a woman, and how, equally, it was responded to. Wherever Emmet is commemorated let Anne Devlin not be forgotten. Bryan Devlin had a dairy farm in Butterfield Lane; his fields are still green there. Five sons of his fought in '98. Anne was his daughter, and she went to keep house for Emmet when he moved into Butterfield

House. You know how she kept vigil there on the night of the rising. When all was lost and Emmet came out in his hurried retreat through Rathfarnham to the mountains, her greeting was according to tradition it was spoken in Irish, and Emmet must have replied in Irish—"Musha, bad welcome to you! Is Ireland lost by you, cowards that you are, to lead the people to destruction and then to leave them?" "Don't blame me, Anne; the fault is not mine," said Emmet. And she was sorry for the pain her words had inflicted, spoken in the pain of her own disappointment. She would have tended him like a mother could he have tarried there, but his path lay to Kilmashogue, and hers was to be a harder duty. When Sirr came out with his soldiery she was still keeping her vigil." Where is Emmet?" "I have nothing to tell you." To all their questions she had but one answer: "I have nothing to say; I have nothing to tell you." They swung her up to a cart and half-hanged her several times; after each half-hanging she was revived and questioned: still the same answer. They pricked her breast with bayonets until the blood spurted out in their faces. They dragged her to prison and tortured her for days. Not one word did they extract from that steadfast woman. And when Emmet was sold, he was sold, not by a woman, but by a man—by the friend that he had trusted—by the counsel who, having sold him, was to go through the ghastly mockery of defending him at the bar.

The fathers and mothers of Ireland should often tell their children that story of Robert Emmet and that story of Anne Devlin. To the Irish mothers who hear me I would say that when at night you kiss your children and in your hearts call down a benediction, you could wish for your boys no higher thing than that, should the need come, they may be given the strength to make Emmet's sacrifice, and for your girls no greater gift from God than such fidelity as Anne Devlin's.

It is more than a hundred years since these things were suffered; and they were suffered in vain if nothing of the spirit of Emmet and Ann Devlin survives in the young men and young women of Ireland. Does anything of that spirit survive? I think I can speak for my own generation. I think I can speak for my contemporaries in the Gaelic League, an organisation which has not yet concerned itself with politics, but whose younger spirits are accepting the full national idea and are bringing into the national struggle the passion and the practicalness which marked the early stages of the language movement. I think I can speak for the young men of the Volunteers. So far, they have no programme beyond learning the trade of arms: a trade which no man of Ireland could learn for over a hundred years past unless he took the English shilling. It is a good programme; and we may almost commit the future of Ireland to the keeping of the Volunteers. I think I can speak for a younger generation still: for some of the young men that are entering the National University, for my own pupils at St. Enda's College, for the boys of Fianna Eireann. To the grey-haired men whom I see on this platform, to John Devoy and Richard Burke, I bring, then, this message from Ireland: that their seed-sowing of forty years ago has not been without its harvest, that there are young men and little boys in Ireland to-day who remember what they taught and who, with God's blessing, will one day take—or make—an opportunity of putting their teaching into practice.

AN ADDENDUM

(AUGUST 1914)

Since I spoke the words here reprinted there has been a quick movement of events in Ireland. The young men of the nation stand organised and disciplined, and are rapidly arming themselves; blood has flowed in Dublin Streets, and the cause of the Volunteers has been consecrated by a holocaust. A European war has brought about a crisis which may contain, as yet hidden within it, the moment for which the generations have been waiting. It remains to be seen whether, if that moment reveals itself, we shall have the sight to see and the courage to do, or whether it shall be written of this generation, alone of all the generations of Ireland, that it had none among it who dared to make the ultimate sacrifice.

THE COMING REVOLUTION

(NOVEMBER 1913)

I have come to the conclusion that the Gaelic League, as the Gaelic League, is a spent force; and I am glad of it. I do not mean that no work remains for the Gaelic League, or that the Gaelic League is no longer equal to work; I mean that the vital work to be done in the new Ireland will be done not so much by the Gaelic League itself as by men and movements that have sprung from the Gaelic League or have received from the Gaelic League a new baptism and a new life of grace. The Gaelic League was no reed shaken by the wind, no mere *vox clamantis*: it was a prophet and more than a prophet. But it was not the Messiah. I do not know if the Messiah has yet come, and I am not sure that there will be any visible and personal Messiah in this redemption: the people itself will perhaps be its own Messiah, the people labouring, scourged, crowned with thorns, agonising and dying, to rise again immortal and impassible. For peoples are divine and are the only things that can properly be spoken of under figures drawn from the divine epos.

If we do not believe in the divinity of our people we have had no business, or very little, all these years in the Gaelic League. In fact, if we had not believed in the divinity of our people, we should in all probability not have gone into the Gaelic League at all. We should have made our peace with the devil, and perhaps might have found him a very decent sort; for he liberally rewards with attorney-generalships, bank balances, villa residences, and so forth, the great and the little who serve him well. Now, we did not turn our backs upon all these desirable things for the sake of *is* and *tá*. We did it for the sake of Ireland. In other words, we had one and all of us (at least, I had, and I hope that all you had) an

45

ulterior motive in joining the Gaelic League. We never meant to be Gaelic Leaguers and nothing more than Gaelic Leaguers. We meant to do something for Ireland, each in his own way. Our Gaelic League time was to be our tutelage: we had first to learn to know Ireland, to read the lineaments of her face, to understand the accents of her voice; to re-possess ourselves, disinherited as we were, of her spirit and mind, re-enter into our mystical birthright. For this we went to school to the Gaelic League. It was a good school, and we love its name and will champion its fame throughout all the days of our later fighting and striving. But we do not propose to remain schoolboys for ever.

I have often said (quoting, I think, Herbert Spencer) that education should be a preparation for complete living; and I say now that our Gaelic League education ought to have been a preparation for our complete living as Irish Nationalists. In proportion as we have been faithful and diligent Gaelic Leaguers, our work as Irish Nationalists (by which term I mean people who accept the ideal of, and work for, the realisation of an Irish Nation, by whatever means) will be earnest and thorough, a valiant and worthy fighting, not the mere carrying out of a ritual. As to what your work as an Irish Nationalist is to be, I cannot conjecture; I know what mine is to be, and would have you know yours and buckle yourself to it. And it may be (nay, it is) that yours and mine will lead us to a common meeting-place, and that on a certain day we shall stand together, with many more beside us, ready for a greater adventure than any of us has yet had, a trial and a triumph to be endured and achieved in common.

This is what I meant when I said that our work henceforward must be done less and less through the Gaelic League and more and more through the groups and the individuals that have arisen, or are arising, out of the Gaelic League. There will be in the Ireland of the next few years a multitudinous activity of Freedom Clubs, Young Republican Parties, Labour Organisations, Socialist Groups, and what not; bewildering enterprises undertaken by sane persons and insane persons, by good men and bad men, many of them seemingly contradictory, some mutually destructive, yet all tending towards a common objective, and that objective: the Irish Revolution.

For if there is one thing that has become plainer than another it is that when the seven men met in O'Connell Street to found the Gaelic League, they were commencing, had there been a Liancourt there to make the epigram, not a revolt, but a revolution. The work of the Gaelic League, its appointed work, was that: and the work is done. To every generation its deed. The deed of the generation that has now reached middle life was the Gaelic League: the beginning of the Irish Revolution. Let our generation not shirk *its* deed, which is to accomplish the revolution.

I believe that the national movement of which the Gaelic League has been the soul has reached the point which O'Connell's movement had reached at the close of the series of monster meetings. Indeed, I believe that our movement reached that point a few years ago say, at the conclusion of the fight for Essential Irish; and I said so at the time. The moment was ripe then for a new Young Ireland Party, with a forward policy; and we have lost much by our hesitation. I propose in all seriousness that we hesitate no longer that we push on. I propose that we leave Conciliation Hall behind us and go into the Irish Confederation.

Whenever Dr. Hyde, at a meeting at which I have had a chance of speaking after him, has produced his dove of peace, I have always been careful to produce my sword; and to tantalise him by saying that the Gaelic League has brought into Ireland "Not Peace, but a Sword." But this does not show any fundamental difference of outlook between my leader and me; for while he is thinking of peace between brother-Irishmen, I am thinking of the sword-point between banded Irishmen and the foreign force that occupies Ireland: and his peace is necessary to my war. It is evident that there can be no peace between the body politic and a foreign substance that has intruded itself into its system: between them war only until the foreign substance is expelled or assimilated.

Whether Home Rule means a loosening or a tightening of England's grip upon Ireland remains yet to be seen. But the coming of Home Rule, if come it does, will make no material difference in the nature of the work that lies before us: it will affect only the means we are to employ, our plan of campaign. There remains, under Home Rule as in its absence, the substantial task of achieving the Irish Nation. I do not think it is going to be achieved without stress and trial, without suffering and blood-shed; at any rate, it is not going to be achieved without *work*. Our business here and now is to get ourselves into harness for such work as has to be done.

I hold that before we can do any work, any *men's* work, we must first realise ourselves as men. Whatever comes to Ireland she needs men. And we of this generation are not in any real sense men, for we suffer things that men do not suffer, and we seek to redress grievances by means which men do not employ. We have, for instance, allowed ourselves to be disarmed; and, now that we have the chance of re-arming, we are not seizing it. Professor Eoin Mac Neill pointed out last week that we have at this moment an opportunity of rectifying the capital error we made when we allowed ourselves to be disarmed; and such opportunities, he reminds us, do not always come back to nations.

A thing that stands demonstrable is that nationhood is not achieved otherwise than in arms: in one or two instances there may have been no actual bloodshed, but the arms were there and the ability to use them. Ireland unarmed will attain just as much freedom as it is convenient for England to give her; Ireland armed will attain ultimately just as much freedom as she wants. These are matters which may not concern the Gaelic League, as a body; but they concern every member of the Gaelic League, and every man and woman of Ireland. I urged much of this five or six years ago in addresses to the Ard-Chraobh: but the League was too busy with resolutions to think of revolution, and the only resolution that a member of the League could not come to was the resolution to be a man. My fellow-Leaguers had not (and have not) apprehended that the thing which cannot defend itself, even though it may wear trousers, is no man.

I am glad, then, that the North has "begun." I am glad that the Orangemen have armed, for it is a goodly thing to see arms in Irish hands. I should like to see the A. O. H. armed. I should like to see the Transport Workers armed. I should like to see any and every body of Irish citizens armed. We must accustom ourselves to the thought of arms, to the sight of arms, to the use of arms. We may make mistakes in the beginning and shoot the wrong people; but bloodshed is a cleansing and a sanctifying thing, and the nation which regards it as the final horror has lost its manhood. There are many things more horrible than bloodshed; and slavery is one of them.

THE PSYCHOLOGY OF A
VOLUNTEER

(JANUARY 1914)

"Mughdhorn" has challenged my psychology as un-Irish. At least, he has challenged as un-Irish the psychology of any man that holds the view that it has not been merely for the sake of saving the Irish language we Leaguers have been working all these years. That is a view which I hold and have promulgated. Hence I take it there is question here of my psychology. It is a little embarrassing to a shy person to have his psychology discussed in public. One feels inclined to protest indignantly with the old lady whom the doctor suspected of appendicitis, explaining to her that it meant inflammation of the appendix. "Why, I haven't *got* such a thing!" She thought he meant a kind of tail. I really shrink from a public investigation into my psychology. Let me see how "Mughdhorn" will like a very tender examination of *his*.

I formally challenge as not only un-Irish, but as diseased, the psychology of the man who holds that Parnell's declaration to the people of Connacht "that he would not have taken off his coat to the land question but that he saw in it a means to rouse the people of Ireland to assert their right to self-government," betrayed the "Palesman[8] addressing the mere Gael," and that it was "supercilious" at that. The declaration in question was one of those four or five illuminating and unforgettable sentences of Parnell's which prove him to have been the

---

[8] An inhabitant of the English Pale, a part of Ireland directly under the control of the English government in the Late Middle Ages, or those Irishmen which may hold English loyalties or sympathies, largely speaking English

one really great Nationalist of his time: the true successor of Tone and Mitchel, though working with such different means. The sentence betrays not the Palesman (whatever that may mean)[9] but the Irish Nationalist. I hold its Nationalism to be authentic, and, further, that there is no other Nationalism than the Nationalism therein implied, i.e., that the nation is more important than any part of the nation. A national leader in a struggle for self-government could not have turned aside from the main issue in order to take up even temporarily any other issue, however important, than the national one, except with the object of strengthening his forces for the main fight—the fight for nationhood. Parnell, as leader of the Irish in their struggle for nationhood, would not have been justified in devoting one hour of his time or one penny of his funds to the land war except as a means to an end. Had Parnell had his way the land war would not have been fought out until the national war had been won; and it is a pity that Parnell had not his way, as we and our children may realise full soon.

I challenge again the Irish psychology of the man who sets up the Gael and the Palesman as opposing forces, with conflicting outlooks. We are all Irish, Leinster-reared or Connacht-reared; your native Irish speaker of Iveragh or Erris is more fully in touch with the spiritual past of Ireland than your Wexfordman or your Kildareman, but your Wexfordman or your Kildareman has other Irish traditions which your Iveraghman or your Errisman has lost. It is a great thing to have heard in childhood the songs of a Tadhg Gaedhealach or to have seen a Raftery or a Colm Wallace; it is an equally great thing to have known old men who fought in Wexford in '98, or to have been nursed by a woman who made bullets for the Fenians. All such memories, old and new, are part of Irish history, and he who would segregate Irish history and Irish men into two sections—Irish-speaking and English-speaking—is not helping toward achieving Ireland a Nation.

Am I a Palesman and is Lord O'Brien of Kilfenora a Gael? I propose that in future we reserve the term Palesman for those who uphold

---

[9] Meaning that the term "Palesman" had become somewhat outdated and only served to divide Irishmen, whereas Pearse proposes the term should be reserved for those Irishmen "who uphold the domination of the English."

the domination of the English in Ireland. I propose also that we substitute for the denominations Gael, Gall, and Gall-Gael the common name of Irishman.

I do not know who among the Gaelic Leaguers that have joined the Volunteers has been foolish enough to suggest that he "cares for the language merely as a sort of stimulant in the fight for nationhood." Certainly not I: I have spent the best fifteen years of my life teaching and working for the idea that the language is an essential part of the nation. I have not modified my attitude in anything that I have recently said or written; I have only confessed (and not for the first time) that in the Gaelic League I have all along been working not for the language merely, but for the nation. I now go further, and say that anyone who has been working for the language merely (if there be any such) has never had the true Gaelic League spirit at all, and though in the Gaelic League has never really been of it. I protest that it was not philology, not folklore, not literature, we went into the Gaelic League to serve, but: Ireland a Nation.

TO THE BOYS OF IRELAND

(FEBRUARY 1914)

We of Na Fianna Eireann, at the beginning of this year 1914, a year which is likely to be momentous in the history of our country, address ourselves to the boys of Ireland and invite them to band themselves with us in a knightly service. We believe that the highest thing anyone can do is to SERVE well and truly, and we purpose to serve Ireland with all our fealty and with all our strength. Two occasions are spoken of in ancient Irish story upon which Irish boys marched to the rescue of their country when it was sore beset once—when Cuchulainn and the boy-troop of Ulster held the frontier until the Ulster heroes rose, and again when the boys of Ireland kept the foreign invaders in check on the shores of Ventry until Fionn had rallied the Fianna: it may be that a similar tale shall be told of us, and that when men come to write the history of the freeing of Ireland they shall have to record that the boys of Na Fianna Eireann stood in the battle-gap until the Volunteers armed.

We believe, as every Irish boy whose heart has not been corrupted by foreign influence must believe, that our country ought to be free. We do not see why Ireland should allow England to govern her, either through Englishmen, as at present, or through Irishmen under an appearance of self-government. We believe that England has no business in this country at all—that Ireland, from the centre to the zenith, belongs to the Irish. Our forefathers believed this and fought for it: Hugh O'Donnell and Hugh O'Neill and Rory O'More and Owen Roe O'Neill: Tone and Emmet and Davis and Mitchel. What was true in their time is still true. Nothing that has happened or that can ever happen can alter the truth of it. Ireland belongs to the Irish. We believe, then, that it is the duty of Irishmen to struggle always, never giving in or growing weary, until they have won back their country again.

The object of Na Fianna Eireann is to train the boys of Ireland to fight Ireland's battle when they are men. In the past the Irish, heroically though they have struggled, have always lost, for want of discipline, for want of military knowledge, for want of plans, for want of leaders. The brave Irish who rose in '98, in '48, and in '67, went down because they were not SOLDIERS: we hope to train Irish boys from their earliest years to be soldiers, not only to know the trade of a soldier—drilling, marching, camping, signalling, scouting, and (when they are old enough) shooting—but also, what is far more important, to understand and prize military discipline and to have a MILITARY SPIRIT. Centuries of oppression and of unsuccessful effort have almost extinguished the military spirit of Ireland: if that were once gone—if Ireland were to become a land of contented slaves—it would be very hard, perhaps impossible, ever to arouse her again. We believe that Na Fianna Eireann have kept the military spirit alive in Ireland during the past four years, and that if the Fianna had not been founded in 1909, the Volunteers of 1913 would never have arisen. In a sense, then, the Fianna have been the pioneers of the Volunteers; and it is from the ranks of the Fianna that the Volunteers must be recruited. This is a special reason why we should be active during 1914. The Fianna will constitute what the old Irish called the MACRADH, or boy-troop, of the Volunteers, and will correspond to what is called in France an Ecole Polytechnique or Military School. As the man who was to lead the armies of France to such glorious victories came forth from the Military School of Brienne, so may the man who shall lead the Irish Volunteers to victory come forth from Na Fianna Eireann.

Our programme includes every element of a military training. We are not mere "Boy Scouts" although we teach and practise the art of scouting. Physical culture, infantry drill, marching, the routine of camp life, semaphore and Morse signalling, scouting in all its branches, elementary tactics, ambulance and first aid, swimming, hurling, and football, are all included in our scheme of training; and opportunity is given to the older boys for bayonet and rifle practice. This does not exhaust our programme, for we believe that mental culture should go hand in hand with physical culture, and we provide instruction in Irish and in Irish history, lectures on historical and literary subjects, and musical and social entertainments as opportunities permit.

Finally, we believe with Thomas Davis that "RIGHTEOUS men" must "make our land a Nation Once Again." Hence we endeavour to train our boys to be pure, truthful, honest, sober, kindly; clean in heart as well as in body; generous in their service to their parents and companions now as we would have them generous in their service to their country hereafter. We bear a very noble name and inherit very noble traditions, for we are called after the Fianna of Fionn, that heroic companionship which, according to legend, flourished in Ireland in the second and third centuries of the Christian era.

"We, the Fianna, never told a lie,
Falsehood was never imputed to us,"

said Oisin to Saint Patrick; and again when Patrick asked Caoilte Mac Ronain how it came that the Fianna won all their battles, Caoilte replied: "Strength that was in our hands, truth that was on our lips, and purity that was in our hearts."

Is it too much to hope that after so many centuries the old ideals are still quick in the heart of Irish youth, and that this year we shall get many hundred Irish boys to come forward and help us to build up a brotherhood of young Irishmen strong of limb, true and pure in tongue and heart, chivalrous, cultured in a really Irish sense, and ready to spend themselves in the service of their country?

SINNE,
NA FIANNA EIREANN.

WHY WE WANT RECRUITS

(MAY 1915)

We want recruits because we have undertaken a service which we believe to be of vital importance to our country, and because that service needs whatever there is of manly stuff in Ireland in order to its effective rendering.

We want recruits because we have a standard to rally them to. It is not a new standard raised for the first time by the men of a new generation. It is an old standard which has been borne by many generations of Irish men, which has gone into many battles, which has looked down upon much glory and upon much sorrow; which has been a sign to be contradicted, but which shall yet shine as a star. There is no other standard in the world so august as the standard we bear; and it is the only standard which the men of Ireland may bear without abandoning their ancient allegiance. Individual Irishmen have sometimes fought under other standards: Ireland as a whole has never fought under any other.

We want recruits because we have a faith to give them and a hope with which to inspire them. They are a faith and a hope which have been handed down from generation to generation of Irish men and women unto this last. The faith is that Ireland is one, that Ireland is inviolate, that Ireland is worthy of all love and all homage and all service that may lawfully be paid to any earthly thing; and the hope is that Ireland may be free. In a human sense, we have no desire, no ambition but the integrity, the honour, and the freedom of our native land.

We want recruits because we are sure of the Tightness of our cause. We have no misgivings, no self-questionings. While others have been

59

doubting, timorous, ill at ease, we have been serenely at peace with our consciences. The recent time of soul-searching had no terrors for us. We saw our path with absolute clearness; we took it with absolute deliberateness. "We could no other." We called upon the names of the great confessors of our national faith, and all was well with us. Whatever soul-searchings there may be among Irish political parties now or hereafter, we go on in the calm certitude of having done the clear, clean, sheer thing. We have the strength and the peace of mind of those who never compromise.

We want recruits because we believe that events are about to place the destinies of Ireland definitely in our hands, and because we want as much help as possible to enable us to bear the burden. The political leadership of Ireland is passing to us—not, perhaps, to us as individuals, for none of us are ambitious for leadership and few of us fit for leadership; but to our party, to men of our way of thinking: that is, to the party and to the men that stand *by Ireland only*, to the party and to the men that stand by the nation, to the party and to the men of one allegiance.

We want recruits because we have work for them to do. We do not propose to keep our men idle. We propose to give them work—hard work, plenty of work. We would band together all men capable of working for Ireland and give them men's work.

We want recruits because we are able to train them. The great majority of our officers are now fully competent to undertake the training of Irish Volunteers for active service under the conditions imposed by the natural and military facts of the map of Ireland. Those officers who are not so competent will be made competent in our training camps during the next few months.

We want recruits because we are able to arm them. In a rough way of speaking, we have succeeded already in placing a gun and ammunition therefor in the hands of every Irish Volunteer that has undertaken to endeavour to pay for them. We are in a position to do as much for every man that joins us. We may not always have the popular pattern of gun, but we undertake to produce a gun of some sort for every genuine Irish Volunteer; with some ammunition to boot. Finally:

We want recruits because we are absolutely determined to take action the moment action becomes a duty. If a moment comes as a moment seemed on the point of coming at least twice during the past eighteen months—when the Irish Volunteers will be justified to their consciences in taking definite military action, such action will be taken. We do not anticipate such a moment in the very near future; but we live at a time when it may come swiftly and terribly. What if Conscription be forced upon Ireland? What if a Unionist or a Coalition British Ministry repudiate the Home Rule Act? What if it be determined to dismember Ireland? What if it be attempted to disarm Ireland? The future is big with these and other possibilities.

And these are among the reasons why we want recruits.

O'DONOVAN ROSSA

A CHARACTER STUDY

O'Donovan Rossa was not the greatest man of the Fenian generation, but he was its most typical man. He was the man that to the masses of his countrymen then and since stood most starkly and plainly for the Fenian idea. More lovable and understandable than the cold and enigmatic Stephens, better known than the shy and sensitive Kickham, more human than the scholarly and chivalrous O'Leary, more picturesque than the able and urbane Luby, older and more prominent than the man who, when the time comes to write his biography, will be recognised as the greatest of the Fenians—John Devoy—Rossa held a unique place in the hearts of Irish men and Irish women. They made songs about him, his very name passed into a proverb. To avow oneself a friend of O'Donovan Rossa meant in the days of our fathers to avow oneself a friend of Ireland; it meant more: it meant to avow oneself a "mere" Irishman, an "Irish enemy," an "Irish savage," if you will, naked and unashamed. Rossa was not only "extreme," but he represented the left wing of the "extremists." Not only would he have Ireland free, but he would have Ireland Gaelic.

And here we have the secret of Rossa's magic, of Rossa's power: he came out of the Gaelic tradition. He was of the Gael; he thought in a Gaelic way; he spoke in Gaelic accents. He was the spiritual and intellectual descendant of Colm Cille and of Seán an Díomais. With Colm Cille he might have said, "If I die it shall be from the love I bear the Gael;" with Shane O'Neill he held it debasing to "twist his mouth with English." To him the Gael and the Gaelic ways were splendid and holy, worthy of all homage and all service; for the English he had a hatred that was tinctured with contempt. He looked upon them as an inferior race, morally and intellectually; he despised their civilisation; he mocked at their institutions and made them look ridiculous.

And this again explains why the English hated him above all the Fenians. They hated him as they hated Shane O'Neill, and as they hated Parnell; but more. For the same "crime" against English law as his associates he was sentenced to a more terrible penalty; and they pursued him into his prison and tried to break his spirit by mean and petty cruelty. He stood up to them and fought them: he made their whole penal system odious and despicable in the eyes of Europe and America. So the English found Rossa in prison a more terrible foe than Rossa at large; and they were glad at last when they had to let him go. Without any literary pretensions, his story of his prison life remains one of the sombre epics of the earthly inferno.

O'Donovan Rossa was not intellectually broad, but he had great intellectual intensity. His mind was like a hot flame. It seared and burned what was base and mean; it bored its way through falsehoods and conventions; it shot upwards, unerringly, to truth and principle. And this man had one of the toughest and most stubborn souls that have ever been. No man, no government, could either break or bend him. Literally he was incapable of compromise. He could not even parley with compromisers. Nay, he could not act, even for the furtherance of objects held in common, with those who did not hold and avow all his objects. It was characteristic of him that he refused to associate himself with the "new departure" by which John Devoy threw the support of the Fenians into the land struggle behind Parnell and Davitt; even though the Fenians compromised nothing and even though their support were to mean (and did mean) the winning of the land war. Parnell and Davitt he distrusted; Home Rulers he always regarded as either foolish or dishonest. He knew only one way; and suspected all those who thought there might be two.

And while Rossa was thus unbending, unbending to the point of impracticability, there was no acerbity in his nature. He was full of a kindly Gaelic glee. The olden life of Munster, in which the *seanchaidhe* told tales in the firelight and songs were made at the autumn harvesting and at the winter spinning, was very dear to him. He saw that life crushed out, or nearly crushed out, in squalor and famine during '47 and '48; but it always lived in his heart. In English prisons and in American cities he remembered the humour and the lore of Carbery. He jested when he was before his judges; he jested when he was tortured by his jailors sometimes he startled the silence of the prison corridors by laughing aloud and by singing Irish songs in his cell: they thought he was going mad, but he was only trying to keep himself sane.

I have heard from John Devoy the story of his first meeting with Rossa in prison. Rossa was being marched into the governor's office as Devoy was being marched out. In the gaunt man that passed him Devoy did not recognise at first the splendid Rossa he had known. Rossa stopped and said, "John." "Who are you?" said Devoy: "I don't know you." "I'm Rossa." Then the warders came between them. Devoy has described another meeting with Rossa, and this time it was Rossa who did not know Devoy. One of the last issues of *The Gaelic American* that the British Government allowed to enter Ireland contained Devoy's account of a recent visit to Rossa in a hospital in Staten Island. It took a little time to make him realise who it was that stood beside his bed." And are you John Devoy?" he said at last. During his long illness he constantly imagined that he was still in an English prison; and there was difficulty in preventing him from trying to make his escape through the window. I have not yet seen any account of his last hours: the cabling of such things would imperil the Defence of the Realm.

Enough to know that that valiant soldier of Ireland is dead; that that unconquered spirit is free.

O'DONOVAN ROSSA

GRAVESIDE PANEGYRIC

'A Ghaedheala,

Do hiarradh orma-sa labhairt indiu ar son a bhfuil cruinnighthe ar an láthair so agus ar son a bhfuil beo de Chlannaibh Gaedheal, ag moladh an leomhain do leagamar i gcré annso agus ag gríosadh meanman na gcarad atá go brónach ina dhiaidh.

A cháirde, ná bíodh brón ar éinne atá ina sheasamh ag an uaigh so, acht bíodh buidheachas againn inar gcroidhthibh do Dhia na ngrás do chruthuigh anam uasal áluinn Dhiarmuda Uí Dhonnabháin Rosa agus thus ré fhada dhó ar an saoghal so.

Ba chalma an fear thú, a Dhiarmuid. Is tréan d'fhearais cath ar son cirt do chine, is ní beag ar fhuilingis; agus ní dhéanfaidh Gaedhil dearmad ort go bráth na breithe.

Acht, a cháirde, ná bíodh brón orainn, acht bíodh misneach inar gcroidhthibh agus bíodh neart inar gcuisleannaibh, óir tuigimís nach mbíonn aon bhás ann nach mbíonn aiséirghe ina dhiaidh, agus gurab as an uaigh so agus as na huaghannaibh atá inar dtimcheall éireochas saoirse Ghaedheal.

In English:

"I was asked to speak to-day on behalf of everyone gathered in this place and on behalf of all living Gaels, to praise the lion that we have buried here and to give courage to the friends who mourn him.

Friends, let no one standing at this grave be sad; rather let our hearts be thankful to the grace of Jesus, who created Jeremiah O'Donovan

67

Rossa's noble beautiful spirit and who blessed him with a long life.

You were a splendid and brave man Jeremiah. Fiercely you waged war for the rights of your race, and no small amount did you suffer; you will never be forgotten.

But, friends, let us not be sad, but let us have courage in our hearts and strength in our arms for let us understand that after all death comes resurrection and that from this grave and the graves surrounding us will rise the freedom of Ireland."

It has seemed right, before we turn away from this place in which we have laid the mortal remains of O'Donovan Rossa, that one among us should, in the name of all, speak the praise of that valiant man, and endeavour to formulate the thought and the hope that are in us as we stand around his grave. And if there is anything that makes it fitting that I, rather than some other, I rather than one of the grey-haired men who were young with him and shared in his labour and in his suffering, should speak here, it is perhaps that I may be taken as speaking on behalf of a new generation that has been re-baptised in the Fenian faith, and that has accepted the responsibility of carrying out the Fenian programme. I propose to you then that, here by the grave of this unrepentant Fenian, we renew our baptismal vows; that, here by the grave of this unconquered and unconquerable man, we ask of God, each one for himself, such unshakable purpose, such high and gallant courage, such unbreakable strength of soul as belonged to O'Donovan Rossa.

Deliberately here we avow ourselves, as he avowed himself in the dock, Irishmen of one allegiance only. We of the Irish Volunteers, and you others who are associated with us in to-day's task and duty, are bound together and must stand together henceforth in brotherly union for the achievement of the freedom of Ireland. And we know only one definition of freedom: it is Tone's definition, it is Mitchel's definition, it is Rossa's definition. Let no man blaspheme the cause that the dead generations of Ireland served by giving it any other name and definition than their name and their definition.

We stand at Rossa's grave not in sadness but rather in exaltation of spirit that it has been given to us to come thus into so close a communion with that brave and splendid Gael. Splendid and holy causes are served by men who are themselves splendid and holy. O'Donovan Rossa was splendid in the proud manhood of him, splendid in the heroic grace of him, splendid in the Gaelic strength and clarity and truth of him. And all that splendour and pride and strength was compatible with a humility and a simplicity of devotion to Ireland, to all that was olden and beautiful and Gaelic in Ireland, the holiness and simplicity of patriotism of a Michael O'Clery or of an Eoghan O'Growney. The clear true eyes of this man almost alone in his day visioned Ireland as we of to-day would surely have her: not free merely, but Gaelic as well; not Gaelic merely, but free as well.

In a closer spiritual communion with him now than ever before or perhaps ever again, in a spiritual communion with those of his day, living and dead, who suffered with him in English prisons, in communion of spirit too with our own dear comrades who suffer in English prisons to-day, and speaking on their behalf as well as our own, we pledge to Ireland our love, and we pledge to English rule in Ireland our hate. This is a place of peace, sacred to the dead, where men should speak with all charity and with all restraint; but I hold it a Christian thing, as O'Donovan Rossa held it, to hate evil, to hate untruth, to hate oppression, and, hating them, to strive to overthrow them. Our foes are strong and wise and wary; but, strong and wise and wary as they are, they cannot undo the miracles of God who ripens in the hearts of young men the seeds sown by the young men of a former generation. And the seeds sown by the young men of '65 and '67 are coming to their miraculous ripening to-day. Rulers and Defenders of Realms had need to be wary if they would guard against such processes. Life springs from death; and from the graves of patriot men and women spring living nations. The Defenders of this Realm have worked well in secret and in the open. They think that they have pacified Ireland. They think that they have purchased half of us and intimidated the other half. They think that they have foreseen everything, think that they have provided against everything; but the fools, the fools, the fools!—they have left us our Fenian dead, and while Ireland holds these graves, Ireland unfree shall never be at peace.

FROM A HERMITAGE

PREFACE

The articles which follow were contributed by me to *Irish Freedom* during the eight months extending from June 1913 to January 1914. They thus form a contemporary commentary on the period immediately preceding and covering the rise of the Irish Volunteers: a period which, when things assume their proper perspective, will probably be regarded as the most important in recent Irish history. I commenced the series with the deliberate intention, by argument, invective, and satire, of goading those who shared my political views to commit themselves definitely to an armed movement. I felt quite sure that the hour was ripe for such a movement, but did not in the beginning foresee the precise form it was to assume. When I wrote the article for November 1913 a group of Nationalists with whom I was in touch had decided to found the Irish Volunteers, and we were looking about for a leader who would command the adhesion of men less "advanced" than we were known to be: of our own followers we were sure. When I wrote the article for December 1913, Eoin MacNeill had (quite unexpectedly) published his article "The North Began" in *An Claidheamh Soluis*, and we had agreed to invite him to put himself at our head. The rest is a part of Irish history.

In the article for August 1913, I have omitted part of the Open Letter to Douglas Hyde; and I have made one or two verbal changes in a few of the other articles.

P. H. PEARSE.

ST. ENDA'S COLLEGE, THE HERMITAGE, RATHFARNHAM,
1st June, 1915.

FROM A HERMITAGE

I

(JUNE 1913)

Not everyone that lives in a hermitage is a hermit. And not every hermit is hermit-hearted. As for me, I have only two qualities in common with the real (or imaginary) hermit who once lived (or did not live) in this place: I am poor and I am merry. Now, all hermits are poor, and all hermits, unless they are frauds, are merry. I am visibly poor, but am merry only in an esoteric or secret sense, exhibiting to the outer world an austerity of lock and speech more befitting my habitation than my heart. Understand that, however harshly I may express myself in the comments and proposals I shall from time to time make here, I am in reality a genial and large-hearted person, and that if I chasten my fellows it is only because I love them.

I have, as I have suggested, some proposals to make. The first is that we who are determined to rehabilitate this nation should commence working towards that end instead of arguing. The Nationalist movement in Ireland has degenerated into a debating society. In all our national or quasi-national organs we argue as to what a nation is, what nationality, what a Nationalist. As if definitions mattered! Our love of disputation sometimes makes us indecent, as when we argue over a dead man's coffin as to whether he was a Nationalist or not, and sometimes makes us ridiculous, as when we prove by a mathematical formula that the poet who has most finely voiced Irish nationalism in our time is no Nationalist. As if a man's opinions were more important than his work! I propose that we take *service* as our touch-stone, and reject all other touchstones; and that, without bothering our heads about sorting out, segregating, and labelling Irishmen and Irishwomen according to their opinions, we agree to accept as fellow-Nationalists all who specifically

72

or virtually recognise this Irish nation as an entity and, being part of it, owe it and give it their service. This will save endless discussion, and make it wholly unnecessary to inquire, before giving a fellow-Irishman one's hand, what is his attitude towards bimetallism or what his opinion of "The Playboy of the Western World."

This thing of service merits to be dwelt upon. Ireland, in our day as in the past, has excommunicated some of those who have served her best, and has canonised some of those who have served her worst. We damn a man for an unpopular phrase; we deify a man who does a mean thing gracefully. The word to us is ever more significant than the deed. When a man like Synge, a man in whose sad heart there glowed a true love of Ireland, one of the two or three men who have in our time made Ireland considerable in the eyes of the world, uses strange symbols which we do not understand, we cry out that he has blasphemed and we proceed to crucify him. When a sleek lawyer, rising step by step through the most ignoble of all professions, attains to a Lord Chancellorship or to an Attorney-Generalship, we confer upon him the freedom of our cities. This is really a very terrible symptom in contemporary Ireland. It is not for me to judge the Redmond Barrys and the Ignatius O'Briens and the Thomas F. Moloneys, and I say no word in condemnation of them here: I merely point out that they have not in any way served Ireland—they have served themselves and they have served England; and when England rewards them for their service there is absolutely no reason why Ireland should rejoice. A bargain has been completed. Servants of England have done their day's work and been paid their price. It is a commercial transaction, not a matter of public rejoicing. It is a business between England and these men. Ireland has nothing to do with it.

When such commercial transactions are concluded I think the less said about them the better. I would not pursue these men as traitors, for I do not think they were ever with us. But I do think that an effort should be made to prevent "rebel" cities like Cork from honouring their mean success. Is it too late, even now, to expunge their names from the roll of freemen? Let someone in Cork look to it.

This generation of Irishmen will be called upon in the near future to make a very passionate assertion of nationality. The form in which that assertion shall be made must depend upon many things, more especially upon the passage or non-passage of the present Home Rule Bill. In the meantime there is need to be vigilant. Yet, every day we allow insults to the nation to pass, forgetting that every fresh stripe endured by a slave makes him so much more a slave. There comes to a slave, as there comes to a tortured child or to a tortured animal, a time when stripes seem normal and it is easier to endure than to protest. Any underling of British government can now lay hands on Ireland with impunity; only now it is no longer necessary to deal heavy stripes—a delicate and facetious slap in the face is a sufficient symbol of over-lordship. One Mr. Justice Boyd sneered at the Irish language from the Bench in Belfast a few weeks ago; one would have thought that there were enough Gaels in Belfast to prevent the fellow from being heard in his own court the next day until he had apologised. The National Council of Sinn Fein recently sent an anti-enlisting car through the streets of Dublin. It was seized by the police and the posters defaced. Afterwards the excuse was tendered that the cart exceeded the size allowed by the Corporation for advertisement vans. The National Council promptly sent another anti-enlisting car, of regulation size, into the streets, and at present it parades unmolested. But there should have been enough spirit in Dublin to enable the National Council to send a whole procession of anti-enlisting cars into the streets. And, had these been seized, a hundred sandwich men should have appeared with anti-enlisting posters. And, had these been interfered with, Nationalist citizens should have set out for business the next morning with anti-enlisting badges in their buttonholes. Should the police have disliked the aesthetic effect of this decoration, neat anti-enlisting flags might have appeared in citizens' hatbands. Should all sartorial eccentricities have been objected to, Nationalist Dublin could have started whistling some tune agreed upon and recognised to mean "anti-enlisting." There are countless ways in which such an agitation might be carried on, for the glory of God and the honour of Ireland. Once for all, if there is to be an anti-enlisting movement, let there be an anti-enlisting movement. Opinions may differ as to the advisability of such a movement, but there can be no two opinions as to the inadvisability of playing at such a movement.

I am aware that some of the courses I recommend are open to the objection that they would land some people in gaol. But gaol would do some people good.

II

(JULY 1913)

Symbols are very important. The symbol a true thing, of a beneficent thing, is worthy of all homage; the symbol of a false thing, of a cruel thing, is worthy of all reprobation. A gibbet has come to be the noblest symbol in the world, because it symbolises the noblest thing that has ever been done among men. The red coat of a soldier, a gallant thing in itself, has come to be a symbol of unspeakably evil import because such unspeakable things have been done by the empire for which the red-coated soldiers fight, such murders perpetrated, such tyrannies upheld for centuries. Thus, a shameful thing may come to have a glorious significance, a ridiculous thing may achieve venerability, while a goodly thing may become so degraded that the stomach of a strong man heaves when he looks upon it. Consider this: if a man were to walk down O'Connell Street wearing a double-pointed conical hat a full foot high and of a glaring yellow colour, we should laugh; yet when a man mounts the steps of an altar with a hat of that precise pattern on his head we are dumb and reverent, for we see in the preposterous headgear the awful symbol of apostolic succession. This matter of symbols came into my mind to-day as I watched a Bishop administer Confirmation. The Church to which I belong, the wise Church that has called into her service all the arts, knows better than any other institution, human or divine, the immense potency of symbols: with symbols she exorcises evil spirits, with symbols she calls into play for beneficent purposes the infinite powers of omnipotence. And those of her children who honour not her symbols she pronounces anathema.

A nation should exact similar respect for its symbols. Free nations do. They salute their flags with bared heads; they hail with thundering cannon the nincompoops that happen to be their kings. A man with whom you would not sit at meat if he were a private individual, whom you would cut every time you saw him approaching you in the street, receives your homage, and justly receives your homage, when he symbolises the majesty of your nation. A man whom, as an individual, you would consider too insignificant to be an object of your dislike, becomes an object of holy hatred when he symbolises some evil thing that oppresses you or yours. No one in Ireland either likes or dislikes George Wettin; yet every true man of Ireland hates, or should hate, to see his not very intellectual features on a coin or on a stamp, for they symbolise there the foreign tyranny that holds us. A good Irishman should blush every time he sees a penny. A good Irishman should tingle with shame every time he sees a red coat.

I know an old woman who never passes a soldier without railing at him. As a girl she made bullets for the Fenians, moulding them out of the leaden lining of tea cases. During the half century that has gone by, while our fathers and we have been parleying with the English, she has cherished in her heart an enduring hate. I saw her a few weeks ago as she went by the Wellington Barracks on her way to the Wolfe Tone Aeridheacht, and as she passed the sentry at the gate she paused and said something bitter to him. I would not have done that. I could not even if I would. Neither could you. A strong man would regard it as futile; a man with a sense of humour would regard it as ridiculous, just as most men regard the demonstrations of the Suffragettes. Yet I think the women are right and not we. At the root of that old woman's demonstration against the stolid sentry was an instinct profoundly true. She is in revolt against the evil thing that holds her country, and of that evil thing the sentry is the symbol. She is an unconquered soul, one of the few unconquered souls in Ireland. She has not made peace, and will never make peace. She has never even parleyed. It were wrong to laugh at her little feeble demonstration against the soldier. I do not call for demonstrations against soldiers until we are able to do more than demonstrate; but the fact that we pass them by every day, every hour, without grinding our teeth is symptomatic of our loss of manhood. We no longer feel their presence here a reproach.

Of the nation's symbols the most august is her language, and it is a measure of Ireland's degradation that she can endure to see her language derided by a Mr. Justice Boyd and that she can discuss the propriety of selling it for £10,000 a year to a Mr. Secretary Birrell. Ireland has lost the sense of shame. Her inner sanctities are no longer sacred to her. Keating (whom I take to be the greatest of Irish Nationalist poets) used a terrific phrase of the Ireland of his day: he called her "the harlot of England." Yet Keating's Ireland was the magnificent Ireland in which Rory O'More planned and Owen Roc battled. What would he say of this Ireland? His phrase if used to-day would no longer be a terrible metaphor, but would be a more terrible truth; a truth literal and exact. For is not Ireland's body given up to the pleasure of another, and is not Ireland's honour for sale in the marketplaces?

As long as Ireland is unfree the only honourable attitude for Irishmen and Irishwomen is an attitude of revolt. It is base of us to be quiescent. It is base not only for the nation, but for each individual in the nation: each of us is guilty of a personal baseness, each of us suffers a personal stigma, as long as this thing endures. When we go to Wolfe Tone's grave next Sunday we should remember with bitterness that we suffer the ignominy which he died rather than endure. If we mean to go on suffering it, we have no business going in pilgrimage to that dead man's grave. If we do not really mean to carry on his work, why disturb the quiet of Bodenstown with protestations?

I said last month that this generation of Irishmen will be called upon in the near future to make a very passionate assertion of nationality, and that the form which that assertion shall take must depend largely upon the passage or non-passage of the present Home Rule Bill. If the Home Rule Bill passes I imagine that the assertion I speak of will be made by the creation of what we may call a Gaelic party within the Home Rule Parliament, with a strong following behind it in the country; a party which shall determinedly set about the rehabilitation of this nation, resting not until it has eliminated every vestige of foreign interference with its concerns. If the Home Rule Bill does not pass (and those who are offering an instalment of liberty to Ireland are proving such bad guardians of liberty in their own country that it is doubtful whether their own countrymen will retain them in office sufficiently long to allow them to pass Home Rule), the assertion must be made in other ways: I believe that if we who hold the full national faith have but the courage to step forward we shall succeed more easily than most people suppose in gaining the people's adhesion to our ideals and our methods—lesser ideals having proved unattainable and wiser methods more foolish.

III

(AUGUST 1913)

Once I knew a Bishop who used to devote the greater part of his spare time to writing Limericks in competition for prizes offered by newspapers. You will find it difficult to imagine a Bishop writing Limericks. One imagines a Bishop in his spare hours writing biblical commentaries or cultivating a neat garden in which the characteristic flower is lily-of-the-valley. And yet my Bishop was a saint. The not very apostolic occupation of his leisure had its origin in an apostolic simplicity and charity. The Bishop had a little niece of whom he was very fond, and the ambition of the little niece's life was to win one of the large prizes offered by London newspapers for clever Limericks. The good Bishop sent in a vast number of Limericks in his niece \s name, and if he or she won a prize (which, I am sorry to say, neither of them ever did), half the money was to be spent in sending the little niece on a pilgrimage to Lourdes and the other half to given to the Society of St. Vincent de Paul. If I had not learned all this from a friend of the little niece's I might have set down the Limerick writing (for some of the Limericks were very bad) as a reprehensible eccentricity on the part of an otherwise excellently behaved Bishop.

At that time I was not a hermit, and was not versed in the wise foolishness of saints. From the Bishop's and from other instances have since elaborated this piece of wisdom: when a good man does an inexplicable thing there is always a motive creditable to his goodness. Men's follies are often more symptomatic of their virtues than of their vices. Apply this to those round about you, your home, in your office, in your organisation: apply it to the busy-bodies and the fools who appear to be making a mess of everything you are interested in, from your breakfast to your country, and you will come to respect them for their very blunders, to love them for their lunacy. You prefer your eggs well boiled. Your wife insists on serving them to you half raw. This is not perverseness on her part: she knows that the albumen of eggs when solidified is highly indigestible and when swallowed hastily every morning, and washed down with tea, will assuredly induce appendicitis. You hate to sit in a draught. The man whose stool is next you in your office insists on keeping a window open from which an atmospheric stream constantly impinges upon your thinly-thatched cranium. This is not cruelty on his part: he knows (being a reader of Lady Aberdeen's *Slainte*) that you are tubercular, and that fresh air is the only thing that will kill the germs. You are a member of the Gaelic League. A friend and colleague writes to the press to point out that you are selling the League to the Liberals and that your reward will be a title. This is not a damned lie: it is his way of hinting that you ought to be a little more strenuous, to smite a little harder and a little oftener, to keep up perpetually a sort of Berserker rage or *riastral* in the way of the old heroes. It is his crude, inartistic, modern notion of playing Laegh to your Cuchulainn. The bravest hero of the Gael had to endure being called "a little fairy phantom" by his charioteer. Were he fighting at the Ford to-day he would be called a "Do-Nothing." When Cuchulainn was reviled by Laegh he did not turn round and fell him. He fought on the harder against the foe of his country.

I love and honour Douglas Hyde. I have served under him since I was a boy. I am willing to serve under him until he can lead and I can serve no longer. I have never failed him. He has never failed me. I am only one of many who could write thus, who at this moment are thinking thus. But probably my service has been longer than that of most, for it began when I was only sixteen; and perhaps it has been more intimate than that of all but a very few, for I have been in posts that required constant communication with him for fifteen years. It has, too, been my privilege to be the first fosterer of many who are now serving under him—pupils of mine, now pupils of his in the National University or young workers in the Gaelic League; and these form a new bond between him and me. Thus by service given and service received I have earned the right to say here the things I am about to say. I can speak to him at once as friend to friend and as loyal soldier to loyal captain.

Or rather, since it has become the fashion to write Open Letters to Douglas Hyde, I will write him an Open Letter. I will commence: "My dear Hyde,—Among God's gracious gifts to you, perhaps the most gracious, at any rate the most useful, is your gift of humour. You have always had a great Homeric laugh. I call upon you to laugh it now. I could show you much matter for laughter in these noises and irrelevancies that disturb you.... Laugh, my dear Craoibhin. Laugh your great genial laugh. It will ease the situation. Bulfin used to say that O'Daly's smile would split the ceiling at 24 Upper O'Connell Street.[10] Let your laughter shake the Clock Tower in Earlsfort Terrace."[11]

To be quite serious, laughter is what is required just now. A shout of laughter that will roll out from the Ard-Fheis at Galway till it re-echoes from the cliffs of Aran and reverberates through the stony solitudes of Burren. Why all this passion of invective when laughter will solve the difficulty? Let us laugh. Laughter is the one gift that God has given to men but denied to brutes and angels. Laughter is the crowning grace of heroes. The epic tells how the dying Cuchulainn noticed that a raven which had looped to drink his blood, becoming entangled in the clotted gore, was ludicrously upset. "Then Cuchulainn, knowing that it was his last laugh, laughed aloud." I think that Emmet, I am quite sure that Tone, would have laughed in similar circumstances.

For my own part, I have found the need of laughter in order to preserve my sanity. And you, Craoibhin, have counselled sanity. There is one piece of sanity that I have learned from being a schoolmaster. Always remember that in a school you have to deal with boys, not cherubim. An enthusiastic teacher often makes the mistake of forming an ideal picture of schoolboy virtue, and is shocked and disheartened

---

[10] Physical headquarters of The Gaelic League.
[11] The Clock Tower has since collapsed.

when he finds that his actual pupils fall far below his ideal. You have, for instance, a little pupil with a virginal face. You say to yourself, "This boy will surely never buy cigarettes in the forbidden shop at the corner, or steal into the garden when the apples are ripe." You come upon him some day in the walk through the wood, and as you approach he hastily conceals a cigarette; you enter the garden in autumn time, and you notice a slight figure with the face of a saint making a dash from the place where the appletrees are. You are angry with the boy, but it is with yourself you should be angry, or rather you should laugh at yourself for a blunderer. The boy has only proved himself a boy, whereas you have proved yourself a goose. Instead of taking down the boy's trousers, you ought to take down the impossible image you had so foolishly erected.

I wonder whether this schoolmaster's wisdom might not be of service to Dr. Hyde. He must try to remember that those around him are men, not archangels. They are men with all the little lovable and unlovable weaknesses of men, and without any of the vision and strength of angels. And he must try to forgive them and to imagine that they mean well even when they act badly; that sometimes at the bottom of their blundering there may be a grain of sense; and that often their fury is only a slightly diseased love of the cause we all serve. And perhaps human causes are best served by men with human strength and human weaknesses. Archangels are fitted to go upon the mighty embassies of God, not to do the little paltry tasks of human life. Archangels are at home in the shining spaces of heaven, not in the habitations and committee rooms of earth. Curious as it seems, we ridiculous men, with all our faults and all our follies, are very capable where angels might fail. Angelic attributes might hinder us in our humble and humdrum but necessary little careers. The inconveniences of being angels on earth would be dreadful. As we sat on our office stools, as we gathered round the table of our committee room, where, for instance, should we tuck in our wings? The buildings would have to be enlarged. In point of fact, a heaven would be necessary to our comfort. But this is earth. And so we are back at our first position that we must put up with our human world and with the human material we have got, until we are all translated and become members of the eternal committee and delegates to the Ard-

Fheis of God.

Thus much to Dr. Hyde. To those on whose behalf I appeal to his magnanimity I say only this: O ye of little sense, know ye not when ye have got a good captain for a good cause? And know ye not that it is the duty of the soldier to follow his captain, unfaltering, unquestioning, "seeing obedience in the bond of rule?" If ye know not this, ye know not the first thing that a fighting man should know.

IV

(SEPTEMBER 1913)

I have been considering the ways of chafers and dragonflies. During the long summer they are my only entertainment in this wilderness. The dragonflies make a pageant for me in the noontide splendour: the chafers are my orchestra in the dusky evening. Marbhén before me was similarly attended:

> "Swarms of bees and chafers, the little musicians of the
> world,
> A gentle chorus."

Your beetle has in him many of the contradictions of the artist. In seemly black, he appeals to you as shy and retiring; suddenly, while you are sympathetically examining him, he splits up the middle, shocking you at first with the indecency of the act, but soon displays hidden wings as though he were an angel in disguise, and then, waving wild arms (like a Yeats making a speech), whirls into ecstasies, and is gone with multitudinous and iridescent whirr of wings and wing-cases. This is nature's symbolling forth of the *divina insania* of the poets. It were perhaps too curious to assign certain beetles to certain poets and dramatists as their types and figures, associating for instance the *Necydalis Major*, long and graceful, with Mr. Yeats, the familiar *Coccinella*, pleasant and comfortable-looking, with Lady Gregory, the

Creophilus Maxillosus, a creature which haunts drains and feeds on garbage (and which I take to be the beetle celebrated in a well-known passage of Keating), with Mr. George Moore.

Upon the dragonfly a literature might be written. The dragonfly is one of the most beautiful and terrible things in nature. It flashes by you like a winged emerald or ruby or turquoise. Scrutinise it at close quarters and you will find yourself comparing its bulky little round head, with its wonderful eyes and cruel jaws, to the beautiful, cruel head of a tiger. The dragonfly among insects is in fact as the tiger among beasts, as the hawk among birds, as the shark among fish, as the lawyer among men, as England among the nations. It is the destroyer, the eater-up, the cannibal. Two dragonflies will fight until nothing remains but two heads. So ferocious an eater-up is the dragonfly that it is said that, in the absence of other bodies to eat up, it will eat up its own body until nothing is left but the head, and it would doubtless eat its own head if it could; a feat which would be as remarkable as the feat of the saint, recorded by Carlyle and recalled by Mitchel, who swam across the Channel carrying his decapitated head in his teeth. The dragonfly is the type of greedy ascendancy—a sinister head preying upon its own vitals. The largest and most wonderful dragonflies I have seen in Ireland haunt the lovely woods that fringe the shore of Lough Corrib, near Cong. And at Cong, I remember, there is a great lord who has pulled down many homes in order that no ascending smoke may mar the sylvan beauty of his landscape.

Of the doings of men only rumours reach me in this solitude. I have heard faint echoes of laughter at Galway, and am pleased to think that the Gael has not entirely lost his sense of humour: a catastrophe which I had feared, for Dr. Hyde had been talking about his aunt's will and Mr. Griffith had been advising Dr. Hyde as to how to conduct a movement to success. The Irish-speaking crowd surging around the brake in Galway square recalls one to the realities of the movement, and to the field that is lying fallow. I want a missionary, a herald, an Irish-speaking John the Baptist, one who would go through the Irish West and speak trumpet-toned of nationality to the people in the villages. I would not have him speak of Gaelic Leagues, or of Fees for Irish, or of Bilingual

Programmes, or of Essential Irish in Universities: I would have him speak of Tone and Mitchel and the Hawk of the Hill and of men dead or in exile for love of the Gael; all in Irish. In the meantime I welcome Eamonn Ceannt and "Bean an Fhir Ruaidh."

Books sometimes find their way to this remote place, and fortunately books, even very profane books, are not forbidden by my rule. This month I have received a good book and a bad book. The good book is indeed one of the holy books of Ireland: no other than John Mitchel's *Jail Journal*, the last gospel of the New Testament of Irish Nationality, as Wolfe Tone's Autobiography is the first; John Mitchel's *Jail Journal* nobly presented, supplemented by an additional chapter of his *Out of Jail Journal*, enriched with good notes and portraits, and introduced by Arthur Griffith in a finely-written preface. Mr. Griffith speaks of the "haughty manhood" of Mitchel. A Man is so rare a phenomenon in Ireland that the appearance of one takes his generation by surprise and he dies broken-hearted or is hanged or transported before his people have made up their minds whether to crown him or to stone him—or simply to ignore him. Mitchel brought reality into a national movement busy with discussions as our own movement is busy with discussions to-day. He admits that he miscalculated: underestimating both "the vigour and zeal" of the enemy and "the much-enduring patience and perseverance" of the Irish. It comes to this: a Man cannot save his people unless the people themselves have some manhood. A Man, even if he be a Man-God, will live and die in vain for all who are voluntary slaves. Christ cannot save you if you want to be damned: much less can any earthly hero.

I agree with one who holds that John Mitchel is Ireland's greatest literary figure—that is, of those who have written in English. But I place Tone above him both as a man and as a leader of men. Tone's was a broader humanity with as intense a nationality; Tone's was a sunnier nature with as stubborn a soul. But Mitchel stands next to Tone: and these two shall teach you and lead you, O Ireland, if you hearken unto them, and not otherwise than as they teach and lead shall you come unto the path of national salvation. For this I will answer on the Judgment Day.

I was wrong in speaking of my second book as a bad book. It is a good book, lovingly written, but it is spoiled by a profane preface. I am speaking of Maurice Moore's life of his father and of George Moore's preface thereto. The soldier has told the facts of his father's life (I wish he had not called him "an Irish Gentleman") simply and well, and the novelist has tried to suggest that his father was not an "Irish gentleman" but an Irish blackguard. Many Irish gentlemen have indeed been blackguards, but I do not think George Henry Moore was one. In a mean and difficult time he worked manfully for Ireland; and towards the end of his life he was willing to become a Fenian. Blackguards do not generally work manfully for their country or become Fenians. But it is absurd and unnecessary to defend George Henry Moore, even against his son. A man's life really speaks for itself, and requires only such faithful record as George Henry Moore's has received here from Maurice Moore. No man's life needs a *Defensio* or an *Apologia*, and I am often sorry to see men really great and simple go to such pains to explain themselves: as if your explanation could make your deeds more eloquent! George Henry Moore was no wrathful and haughty Mitchel, no gay and heroic Tone; but he was a very worthy and gallant figure in his time, and might have served Ireland well if he had learned to know her sooner.

V

(OCTOBER 1913)

It is not amusing to be hungry; at least (for I desire to be moderate in my language), it is not very amusing. Though hunger be proverbially good sauce, one may have too much of it, as of most good things; and, while meat without sauce is tolerable, sauce without meat is apt to pall. Yorkshire Relish (I am told) is delicious, but one would not care to dine upon it. Hunger Sauce must be still less sustaining. Indeed, the only advantage that Hunger Sauce seems to possess over other brands is its extreme cheapness. The very poorest can enjoy it, and it is one of the few luxuries that the rich will not grudge them. But, as far as nutritious properties are concerned, the cakes recommended by Marie Antoinette to the starving peasants of France, in lieu of bread, were preferable. "Why are the people crying?" "Your Majesty, they have no bread." "But why not eat cake?" asked the Queen.

Poor Marie Antoinette did not quite grasp the situation in France. In the end they grasped *her* and hurried her to the guillotine. If Marie Antoinette could have got at the peasant's point of view there might have been no French Revolution. There are only two ways of righting wrongs: reform and revolution. Reform is possible when those who inflict the wrong can be got to see things from the point of view of those who suffer the wrong. Some men can see from other men's points of view by sympathy; most men cannot until you actually put them in the other men's shoes. I would like to put some of our well-fed citizens in the shoes of our hungry citizens, just for an experiment. I would try the hunger cure upon them. It is known that hunger is a good sauce; it is also known that what is sauce for the goose is sauce for the gander. It is further known that a pound a week is sufficient to sustain a Dublin family in honest hunger—at least very rich men tell us so, and very rich men know all about everything, from art galleries to the domestic economy of the tenement room. I would ask those who know that a man can live and thrive, can house, feed, clothe, and educate a large family on a pound a week to try the experiment themselves. Let them show us how the thing is done. We will allow them a pound a week for the sustenance of themselves and their families, and will require them to hand over their surplus income, over and above a pound a week, to some benevolent object. I am quite certain that they will enjoy their poverty and their hunger. They will go about with beaming faces; they will wear spruce and well-brushed clothes; they will drink their black tea with gusto and masticate their dry bread scientifically (Lady Aberdeen will tell them the proper number of bites per slice); they will write books on "How to be Happy though Hungry;" when their children cry for more food they will smile; when their landlord calls for the rent they will embrace him; when their house falls upon them they will thank God; when policemen smash in their skulls they will kiss the chastening baton. They will do all these things—perhaps; in the alternative they may come to see that there is something to be said for the hungry man's hazy idea that there is something wrong somewhere.

It is, of course, easy for me, a well-fed hermit, to write with detachment about hunger. It is always easy for well-fed persons to take detached views of such things; indeed, sometimes the views of the well-fed on these matters are so detached from their subject as to have no relation to it at all. If I were hungry, I should probably write with a little more passion than I am displaying. Indeed, if I were as hungry at this moment as many equally good men of Ireland undoubtedly are, it is probable that I should not be sitting here wielding this pen; possibly I should be in the streets wielding a paving-stone. I frankly admit that I am well-fed; but you must not imagine me a sybarite. Being a hermit, I limit myself to four square meals a day, except on feast-days when, for the greater glory of God, I allow myself five. If I were not thus explicit my views on economic questions might be discounted; I should be described as belonging to the "lowest stratum" of society, and therefore not in any real sense a member of society, or indeed of the human race, at all; it would be hinted that I am a "loafer," that I frequent "street corners," that I am a " socialist," a "syndicalist," and other weird things. I once took a modest part in breaking up a meeting in the Antient Concert Rooms. The next day the *Independent* called me an "unwashed youth." A youth I certainly was, but I had washed myself with scrupulous care that blessed morning; indeed, it is my habit to wash myself in the mornings. A distinguished scholar (now a Professor of the National University) and a distinguished woman of letters (now prominent in the counsels of the United Irishwomen) were beside me on that occasion, and they, too, were described as "unwashed youths:" the words "of both sexes" were added, lest it might be left open to inference that even the ladies who disagree with the *Independent* are so virtuous as to wash themselves. When, therefore, you differ in opinion from a newspaper it is always well to let it be known that you wash yourself regularly, that you take the normal number of meals, that you pay your rent and taxes, that you go to church or chapel, and that, in short, you conform in all particulars to the lofty standard of conduct set up by such an eminent fellow-citizen of yours as Mr. William M. Murphy.

Personally, I am in a position to protest my respectability. I do all the orthodox things. My wild oats were sown and reaped years ago. I am nothing so new-fangled as a socialist or a syndicalist. I am old-fashioned enough to be both a Catholic and a Nationalist. I am not smarting under any burning personal wrong—except the personal wrong I endure in being a member of an enslaved nation. I am at peace with all the men of Ireland. It becomes both my character and my profession to be at peace with my fellow-slaves, whether capitalist or worker, whether rich or poor, whether fed or hungry. God knows that we, poor remnant of a gallant nation, endure enough shame in common to make us brothers. And yet here is a matter in which I cannot rest neutral. My instinct is with the landless man against the lord of lands, and with the breadless man against the master of millions. I may be wrong, but I do hold it a most terrible sin that there should be landless men in this island of waste yet fertile valleys, and that there should be breadless men in this city where great fortunes are made and enjoyed.

I calculate that one-third of the people of Dublin are underfed; that half the children ending Irish primary schools are ill-nourished. Inspectors of the National Board will tell you that there is no use in visiting primary schools in Ireland after one or two in the afternoon: the children are too weak and drowsy with hunger to be capable of answering intelligently. I suppose there are twenty thousand families in Dublin in whose domestic economy milk and butter are all but unknown: black tea and dry bread are their staple articles of diet. There are many thousand fireless hearth-places in Dublin on the bitterest days of winter; there would be many thousand more only for such bodies as the Society of St. Vincent de Paul. Twenty thousand Dublin families live in one-room tenements. It is common to find two or three families occupying the same room; and sometimes one of the families will have a lodger! There are tenement rooms in Dublin in which over a dozen persons live, eat, and sleep. High rents are paid for these rooms, rents which in cities like Birmingham would command neat four-roomed cottages with gardens. The tenement houses of Dublin are so rotten that they periodically collapse upon their inhabitants, and if the inhabitants collect in the streets to discuss matters the police baton them to death.

These are among the grievances against which men in Dublin are beginning to protest. Can you wonder that protest is at last made? Can you wonder that the protest is crude and bloody? I do not know whether the methods of Mr. James Larkin are wise methods or unwise methods (unwise, I think, in some respects), but this I know, that here is a most hideous wrong to be righted, and that the man who attempts honestly to right it is a good man and a brave man.

Poverty, starvation, social unrest, crime, are incidental to the civilisation of such states as England and America, where immense masses of people are herded into great Christless cities and the bodies and souls of men are exploited in the interests of wealth. But these conditions do not to any extent exist in Ireland. We have not great cities; we have not dense industrial populations; we have hardly any ruthless capitalists exploiting immense masses of men. Yet in Ireland we have dire and desperate poverty; we have starvation; we have social unrest. Ireland is capable of feeding twenty million people; we are barely four million. Why do so many of us starve?

Before God, I believe that the root of the matter lies in foreign domination. A free Ireland would not, and could not, have hunger in her fertile vales and squalor in her cities. Ireland has resources to feed five times her population: a free Ireland would make those resources available. A free Ireland would drain the bogs, would harness the rivers, would plant the wastes, would nationalise the railways and waterways, would improve agriculture, would protect fisheries, would foster industries, would promote commerce, would diminish extravagant expenditure (as on needless judges and policemen), would beautify the cities, would educate the workers (and also the non-workers, who stand in direr need of it), would, in short, govern herself as no external power— nay, not even a government of angels and archangels—could govern her. For freedom is the condition of sane life, and in slavery, if we have not death, we have the more evil thing which the poet has named Death-in-Life. The most awful wars are the wars that take place in dead or quasi-dead bodies when the fearsome things that death breeds go forth to prey upon one another and upon the body that is their parent.

VI

(NOVEMBER 1913)

There are incongruities which are humorous, and there are incongruities which are disgusting. All humour has its source in incongruity, but so has all sin. Sometimes the humour of an incongruity is so great that we overlook the fact of its wickedness; sometimes the wickedness of an incongruity is so apparent that only a saint can laugh at its humour (for your saint laughs at things whereat your man of less sanctity, which means of less charity and less humility, is scandalised). There are obvious incongruities at which everyone, from a saint to a solicitor, will at least smile. Thus, when one hears a noble air of Gounod's sung to such words as "My wife stole a hell of a lump of beef;" when one meets an archbishop in gaiters wheeling a perambulator containing his offspring, when one comes upon a bull in a china shop or upon a member of the Chamber of Commerce in an art gallery, one smiles no matter how respectable one is. No question of ethics enters into these cases. It is a pity that a Gounod march should be sung to profane words; but Gounod would suffer no diminution of just fame if all the kleptomaniac exploits of all the wives of the world were chanted to his music. One may have rigid ideas as to the impropriety of archbishops wheeling their offspring in perambulators—and it is certainly going too far to wear gaiters while doing so unarchiepiscopal a thing; but it is not a very serious sin, if sin at all. A bull in a china shop may break a good deal of crockery, but he can hardly break any of the Commandments; and a member of the Chamber of Commerce in an art gallery will not do the pictures any harm, nor, unless he be as sensitive as some Gaelic Leaguers I have known (and that is impossible), will the pictures do him any harm. In these instances nothing suffers but the Law of Congruity; and laws have made so many people suffer that one can well tolerate the notion of a law suffering once in a way.

But there are incongruities which disgust, or at any rate ought to disgust. A millionaire promoting Universal Peace is such an incongruity;

an employer who accepts the aid of foreign bayonets to enforce a lockout of his workmen and accuses the workmen of national dereliction because they accept foreign alms for their starving wives and children, is such an incongruity; a public body in an enslaved country which passes a resolution congratulating a citizen upon selling himself to the enemies of that country, and upon making a good bargain of it, is such an incongruity; an Irish Nationalist, unable to pull the trigger of a gun himself, who sneers at the drillings and rifle practices of Orangemen, is such an incongruity. The Eastern and the Western Worlds are indeed full of incongruities of this sort; each of them matter for a play by a Synge.

To dilate a little on one of them. It is now the creed of Irish nationalism (or at least of that Irish nationalism which is vocal on platforms and in the press) that the possession of arms and a knowledge of the use of arms is a fit subject for satire. To have a rifle is as ridiculous as to have a pimple at the end of your nose, or a bailiff waiting for you round the corner. To be able to use a rifle is an accomplishment as futile as to be able to stand on your head to be able to wag your ears. This is not the creed of any other nationalism that exists or has ever existed in any community, civilised or uncivilised, that has ever inhabited the globe. It has never been the creed of Irish nationalism until this our day. Mitchel and the great confessors of Irish nationalism would have laughed it to scorn. Mitchel, indeed, did laugh to scorn a similar but much less foolish doctrine of O'Connell's; and the generation that came after O'Connell rejected his doctrine and accepted Mitchel's. The present generation of Irish Nationalists is not only unfamiliar with arms but despises all who are familiar with arms. Irish Nationalists share with certain millionaires the distinction of being the only people who believe in Universal Peace—here and now. Even the Socialists who want Universal Peace propose to reach it by Universal War; and so far they are sensible.

It is symptomatic of the attitude of the Irish Nationalist that when he ridicules the Orangeman he ridicules him not for his numerous foolish beliefs, but for his readiness to fight in defence of those beliefs. But this is exactly wrong. The Orangeman is ridiculous in so far as he believes incredible things; he is estimable in so far as he is willing and able to fight in defence of what he believes. It is foolish of an Orangeman to believe that his personal liberty is threatened by Home Rule; but, granting that he believes that, it is not only in the highest degree common sense but it is his clear duty to arm in defence of his threatened liberty. Personally, I think the Orangeman with a rifle a much less ridiculous figure than the Nationalist without a rifle; and the Orangeman who can fire a gun will certainly count for more in the end than the Nationalist who can do nothing cleverer than make a pun. The superseded Italian rifles which the Orangemen have imported may not be very dangerous weapons; but at least they are more dangerous than epigrams. When the Orangemen "line the last ditch" they may make a very sorry show; but we shall make an even sorrier show, for we shall have to get Gordon Highlanders to line the ditch for us.

I am not defending the Orangeman; I am only showing that his condemnation does not lie in the mouth of an unarmed Nationalist. The Orangeman is a sufficiently funny person; and he is funny mainly because he is so serious. He has no sense of incongruity; in his mind's eye he sees without smiling Cardinal Logue sending Protestant worthies to the stake and Sir Edward Carson undergoing the fatigues of a campaign—things which will never be. At least, I think not; for Cardinal Logue is kindly and humorous, and Sir Edward Carson is a lawyer with a price. The Orangeman's lack of a sense of the incongruous is sometimes painful. In Belfast they are selling chair cushions with Sir Edward Carson's head embroidered upon them; which is pretty much as if a man were to emblazon the arms of his country upon the seat of his trousers. One should not put a sacred emblem where it is certain to be sat upon and liable to be kicked; and only Orangemen would think of honouring their chief by sitting on his head.

But the rifles of the Orangemen give dignity even to their folly. The rifles are bound to be useful some day. At the worst they may hasten Sir Edward Carson's final exit from Ulster; at the best they may crack outside Dublin Castle. The Editor of *Sinn Féin* wrote the other day that when the Orangemen fire upon the King of England's troops it will become the duty of every Nationalist in Ireland to join them: there is a deal of wisdom in the thought as well as a deal of humour. Or negotiations might be opened with the Orangemen on these lines: You are erecting a Provisional Government of Ulster—make it a Provisional Government of Ireland and we will recognise and obey it. O'Connell said long ago that he would rather be ruled by the old Protestant Ascendancy Irish Parliament than by the Union Parliament; "and O'Connell was right," said Mitchel. He certainly was. It is unquestionable that Sir Edward Carson's Provisional Government would govern Ireland better than she has been governed by the English Cabinet; at any rate, it could not well govern her worse. Any six Irishmen would be a better Government of Ireland than the English Cabinet has been: any six criminals from Mountjoy Prison, any six lunatics from the Richmond Asylum, any six Orangemen from Portadown. The Irishmen would at least try to govern Ireland in the interests of Irish criminals, lunatics, or Orangemen, as the case might be: the English have governed her in the interests of England. Better exploit Ireland for the benefit of Belfast than exploit her for the benefit of Westminster. Better wipe out Ireland in one year's civil war than let England slowly bleed her to death.

A rapprochement between Orangemen and Nationalists would be difficult. The chief obstacles are the Orangeman's lack of humour and the Nationalist's lack of guns: each would be at a disadvantage in a conference. But a sense of humour can be cultivated, and guns can be purchased. One great source of misunderstanding has now disappeared: it has become clear within the last few years that the Orangeman is no more loyal to England than we are. He wants the Union because he imagines that it secures his prosperity; but he is ready to fire on the Union flag the moment it threatens his prosperity. The position is perfectly plain and understandable. Foolish notions of loyalty to England being eliminated, it is a matter for business-like negotiation. A Nationalist mission to North-East Ulster would possibly effect some good. The case might be put thus: Hitherto England has governed Ireland through the Orange Lodges; she now proposes to govern Ireland through the A. O. H. You object: so do we. Why not unite and get rid of the English? They are the real difficulty; their presence here the real incongruity.

VII

(DECEMBER 1913)

I was once stranded on a desert island with a single companion. When two people are stranded on a desert island they naturally converse. We conversed. We sat on a stony beach and talked for hours. When we had exhausted all the unimportant subjects either of us could think of, we commenced to talk about important subjects. (I have observed that even on a desert island it is not considered good form to talk of important things while unimportant things remain to be discussed.) We had very different points of views, and very different temperaments. I was a boy; my companion was an old man. I was about to enter the most wicked of all professions; my companion was a priest. Being young, I was serious and conceited; being old, my companion was gay and humble. In some respects I was more learned than he: he was trying to spell his way through Keatings *Trí Bior-Ghaoìthe an Bháis*, and I was able to help him. But in every respect he was wiser beyond telling than I, for his life had been stormy and sorrowful, and withal very saintly, so that he had garnered much of the wisdom both of heaven and of earth; and I had garnered only the wisdom of the Board of Intermediate Education. We were thus as singularly ill-assorted a pair as ever sat down together on the beach of a desert island.

Yet we had one interest in common. There was at the bottom of my heart a memory which a course of Intermediate education (by some miracle of God's) had not altogether obliterated. I had heard in childhood of the Fenians from one who, although a woman, had shared their hopes and disappointment. The names of Stephens and O'Donovan Rossa were familiar to me, and they seemed to me the most gallant of all names: names which should be put into songs and sung proudly to tramping music. Indeed, my mother (although she was not old enough to remember the Fenians) used to sing of them in words learned, I daresay, from that other who had known them; one of her songs had the lines—

"Because I was O'Donovan Rossa,
    And a son of Gráinne Mhaol;"

and although I did not quite know who O'Donovan Rossa was or what
his deed had been, I felt that he must have been a gallant and kingly man
and his deed a man's deed. Alice Milligan had not yet made the ballad
of "Owen Who Died," which was to give these heroic names a place in
literature—

"You have heard of O'Donovan Rossa
    From nigh Skibbereen;
You have heard o' the Hawk 'o the Hill-top,
    If you have not seen;
You have heard of the Reaper whose reaping
    Was of grain half green:
Such were the men among us
    In the days that have been."

None of my schoolfellows had ever heard of those names; and if our
masters had heard them they never mentioned them. O'Connell we
heard about; and one day that stands out in my memory, Parnell's name
was mentioned, for a master came into the room and said: "Well, boys,
they say Parnell is dead—the dirty fellow." We all grew very still, for
we were all Parnellites; and we wondered why he should be called a dirty
fellow, and thought it a cruel thing. That was before the Juggernaut car
of the Intermediate had rolled over us, and we still retained most of the
decent kindly instincts with which we had been born. Had it happened
four years later we should probably have applauded the master's
announcement as rather neatly put.

But behold me on the beach of my desert island with my priest
beside me. And my priest, as I found out when we began to talk about
serious things, had known the Fenians, had made something of a stir in
Fenian times, had even been called the Fenian priest! I do not know
whether he had ever been a Fenian; but I know that all the Fenians of a

countryside used to go to confession to him in preference to their own parish priests; and it was said that he had a Sodality of the Sacred Heart composed to a man of sworn Fenians: probably an exaggeration. But this I can vouch for, that he loved the name and fame of the Fenians, and he spoke to me, till his voice grew husky and his eyes filled with tears, of their courage, of their loyalty, of their enthusiasm, of their hope, of their failure. "Stephens should have given the word," he said; "we'll never be as ready as we were the night he escaped from Richmond Prison. We've lost our manhood since." It was the first year of the Boer War. "Look at the chance we have now," he exclaimed: "the British army at the other end of the earth, and one blow would give us Ireland; but we've neither men nor guns. GOD ALMIGHTY WON'T GO ON GIVING US CHANCES if we let every chance slip. You can't expect He'll give us more chances than He gave the Jews. He'll turn His back on us.... And why," he added, "should a lot of old women be free, anyhow?" The worthy man had not considered the Suffragist claim; or perhaps he would have allowed freedom to *bona fide* old women and denied it to old-womanlike young men—in which he would have been right.

For, after all, may it not be said with entire truth that the reason why Ireland is not free is that Ireland has not deserved to be free? Men who have ceased to be men cannot claim the rights of men; and men who have suffered themselves to be deprived of their manhood have suffered the greatest of all indignities and deserved the most shameful of all penalties. It has been sung in savage and exultant verse of a fierce Western clan that its men allowed themselves to be deprived of their sight by a triumphant foe rather than be deprived of their manhood; and it was a man's choice. But modern Irishmen with eyes open have allowed themselves to be deprived of their manhood; and many of them have reached the terrible depth of degradation in which a man will boast of his unmanliness. For in suffering ourselves to be disarmed, in acquiescing in a perpetual disarmament, in neglecting every chance of arming, in sneering (as all Nationalists do now) at those who have taken arms, we in effect abnegate our manhood. Unable to exercise men's rights, we do not deserve men's privileges. We are, in a strict sense, not fit for freedom; and freedom we shall never attain.

It is not reasonable to expect that the Almighty will repeal all the laws of His universe in our behalf. The condition on which freedom is given to men is that they are able to make good their claim to it; and unarmed men cannot make good their claim to anything which armed men choose to deny them. One of the sins against faith is presumption, which is defined as a foolish expectation of salvation without making use of the necessary means to obtain it: surely it is a sin against national faith to expect national freedom without adopting the necessary means to win and keep it. And I know of no other way than the way of the sword: history records no other, reason and experience suggest no other. When I say the sword I do not mean necessarily the actual use of the sword: I mean readiness and ability to use the sword. Which, translated into terms of modern life, means readiness and ability to shoot.

I regard the armed Orangemen of North-East Ulster as potentially the most useful body of citizens Ireland possesses. In fact, they are the only citizens Ireland does possess at this moment: the rest of us for the most part do not count. A citizen who cannot vindicate his citizenship is a contradiction in terms. A citizen without arms is like a priest without religion, like a woman without chastity, like a man without manhood. The very conception of an unarmed citizen is a purely modern one, and even in modern times it is chiefly confined to the populations of the (so-called) British Islands. Most other peoples, civilised and uncivilised, are armed. This is a truth which we of Ireland must grasp. We must try to realise that we are collectively and individually living in a state of degradation as long as we remain unarmed. I do not content myself with saying in general terms that the Irish should arm. I say to each one of you who read this that it is YOUR duty to arm. Until you have armed yourself and made yourself skillful in the use of your arms you have no right to a voice in any concern of the Irish Nation, no right to consider yourself a member of the Irish Nation or of any nation; no right to raise your head among any body of decent men. Arm. If you cannot arm otherwise than by joining Carson's Volunteers, join Carson's Volunteers. But you can, for instance, start Volunteers of your own.

My priest on my desert island spoke to me glowingly about the Three who died at Manchester. He spoke to me, too, of the rescue of

Kelly and Deasy from the prison van and of the ring of armed Fenians keeping the Englishry at bay. I have often thought that that was the most memorable moment in recent Irish history: and that that ring of Irishmen spitting fire from revolver barrels, while an English mob cowered out of range, might well serve as a symbol of the Ireland that should be; of the Ireland that shall be. Next Sunday we shall pay homage to them and to their deed; were it not a fitting day for each of us to resolve that we, too, will be men.

VIII

(JANUARY 1914)

It has penetrated to this quiet place that some of the young men of Ireland have banded themselves together under the noble name of Irish Volunteers with intent to arm in their country's service. I am inclined to doubt the rumour. It has an air of inherent improbability. I could have believed such a report of any generation of young Irishmen of which I have read; but of the generation that I have known I hesitate to believe it. It is not like what they would do. Previous generations of young Irishmen (if what our fathers have told us be true) were foolish and hot-headed, not to say wicked and irreligious. Of course, they had not been properly instructed. Intermediate Boards and National Universities were yet in the womb of the British Government. The expansive power of gunpowder and the immense momentum which can be acquired by a bullet discharged from a gun were not generally known until Natural Philosophy became a subject for Matriculation, and Kennedy published a one-and-sixpenny text-book on the subject: hence our forefathers did not realise how dangerous it is to let off firearms—how could they be expected to? This fact, not hitherto adverted to by historians, goes far to explain the otherwise inexplicable action of the Volunteers of 1778, of the insurgents of 1798, of the Fenians of 1867; men, apparently sane, who expended quite a lot of money on buying or manufacturing deadly arms. Had they realised that the weapons might kill the poor soldiers who were guarding their country, it is unquestionable that they would not have been so inhumane as to procure them. Again, former generations of young Irishmen had no sound notions as to what is proper and gentlemanly. They always failed to recognise that it is not respectable to get yourself hanged, and could never be got to see that prison clothes, no matter how well-made, are not becoming. Robert Emmet was actually guilty of the impropriety of smiling on the scaffold; and surely it was very near blasphemy for three Irish murderers, with manacled hands uplifted from an English dock, to call upon God to "save Ireland" as if that were not the job of the British Government.

Fortunately, we live in a more cultured as well as in a more religious age. We have studied Dynamics and know that firearms are dangerous; we have studied Political Economy and know that it is bad economy to expend money upon a national armament, seeing that we already pay the British Army to fight for us; we have studied Ethics and know that it is unlawful to rise against an established government. We have also cultivated a sense of decorum and a sense of humour. We see that militarism is not only wrong but, what is worse, ridiculous; and we should (very properly) hesitate to go out drilling lest they might put a caricature of us in *Punch*.

My knowledge that all this is so makes me doubt the rumour that a considerable number of young Irishmen have resolved to take arms and to train themselves in the use of arms. The improbability is increased when I come to examine the details of the report. Thus, a Provisional Committee including university professors, schoolmasters, solicitors, barristers, journalists, aldermen, public servants, commercial men, and gentlemen of leisure, is spoken of. I have never known persons of that sort to do anything more exciting than talk over tea and scones in the D. B. C. There are among those classes in Dublin many who are quite fearless—in debate; many who are extraordinarily prompt—in retort; a few who are really able and vigorous—in smashing their opponents' arguments. That such men would turn aside from the realities of dialectics to the theatricalities of military preparation seems highly improbable. When it is added that the Provisional Committee includes United Irish Leaguers, Hibernians, Sinn Féiners, Gaelic Leaguers, and even a few who call themselves simply Separatists, the untruth of the whole story becomes almost manifest; for it is well known that there never has been and that there never can be anything like cordial co-operation between such widely-differing sections of politicians and non-politicians in Ireland. I dismiss therefore the tale of a huge tumultuous meeting of seven or eight thousand people in the largest hall in Dublin, with immense overflow meetings in neighbouring buildings and gardens; the detailed accounts of nightly drillings in various halls; the absurd rumour that Galway (well known to have no other interest than racing, fishing, and British tourists) and Cork (which is prepared to fight all Ireland on the question of conciliation) have flung themselves into the movement; and finally the grotesque fable that young men who are eating their way to the bar or preparing to purchase dispensary appointments from Boards of Guardians have paused in their honourable careers in order to learn how to shoot. These things have happened in other countries and in other times; but surely not in our own country and in our own time.

Consider the dislocating effect of such a movement. In the first place, it would make Home Rule, now about to be abandoned in deference to armed Ulster, almost a certainty; in a second place, should Home Rule miscarry, it would give us a policy to fall back upon. Again, it would make men and citizens of us, whereas we are quite comfortable as old women and slaves. Furthermore, it would unite us in one all-Ireland movement of brotherly co-operation, whereas we derive infinite pleasure from quarrelling with one another. The comfortable feeling that we are safe behind the guns of the British Army, like an infant in its mother's arms, the precious liberty of confuting one another before the British public and thus gaining empire-wide reputations for caustic Celtic humour and brilliant Celtic repartee—these are things that we will not lightly sacrifice. For these privileges have we not cheerfully allowed our population to be halved and our taxation to be quadrupled? Enough said. Volunteering is undesirable. Volunteering is impossible. Volunteering is dangerous.

IX

(JANUARY 1914)

It would appear that the impossible has happened (as, indeed, when one comes to think of the matter, it nearly always does), and that the young men of Ireland are learning again the noble trade of arms. They had almost forgotten that it *was* a noble trade; and when the young men of a nation have reached so terrible a depth as to be unconscious of the dignity of arms, one will naturally doubt their capacity for any virile thought, let alone any virile action. Hence my scepticism of last month. I who am as a babe, believing all things and hoping all things, felt it difficult to believe this. One is disillusioned so often. Once when I was a boy a ballad-singer came to the farmhouse in which I was living for a time in a glen of the Dublin hills. He had ballads of "Bold Robert Emmet" and "Here's a Song for Young Wolfe Tone;" and he told me that in secret places of the hills Fenians had drilled and, for all he knew, were drilling still. So I fared forth in quest of them, trudging along mountain roads at night, full of the faith that in some moonlit glen I should come upon the Fenians drilling. But I never found them. Nowhere beneath the moon were there armed men wheeling and marching. The mountains were lonely. When I came home I said to my grandfather (who had himself been a Fenian, albeit I knew it not), "The Fenians are all dead." "Oh, be the!" said he (his oaths never got further than "be the"), "how do you know that?" "I have gone through all the glens," I answered, "and there were none drilling: they must be dead."

And my naive deduction was very nearly right. If the Fenians were not all dead, the Fenian spirit was dead, or almost dead. By the Fenian spirit I mean not so much the spirit of a particular generation as that virile fighting faith which has been the salt of all the generations in Ireland unto this last. And is it here even in this last? Yea, its seeds are here, and behold they are kindling: it is for you and me to fan them into such a flame as shall consume everything that is mean and compromising and insincere in Ireland and in each man of Ireland—for in every one of us there is much that is mean and compromising and insincere, much that were better burned out. When we stand armed as Volunteers we shall at least be men, and so shall be able to come into communion of thought and action with the virile generations of Ireland: to our betterment, be sure.

The only question that need trouble us now is this: Will the young men of Ireland rise to the opportunity that is given them? They have a year before them: the momentous year of 1914. The fate of the Irish movement in our time will very likely be determined during the coming twelve months, and it will be determined largely by the way in which the Volunteer movement develops. In other words, it will depend upon the young men who have volunteered, for they have the making of the movement in their hands. This is a problem in which the British Government is not a factor; in which the Irish leaders—Parliamentarian, Sinn Féin, Separatist, Gaelic League—are not factors; the young men of the towns and countrysides are the only factors; they and whatever manly stuff is in them. It is a great opportunity for the young men of a people to get. A year is theirs in which to make history.

A former generation of Irishmen got such a year and used it well. An army of 100,000 drilled and equipped men was its glorious fruit. Can we of the twentieth century work to similar purpose and with similar result during the year that has been given to us? I believe we can. There are circumstances which seem to me to make our task easier than theirs.

In the first place, we are poorer than they were. Therefore we shall be more generous. There were many men of money among the Volunteers of 1778-83: it was one of the weaknesses of the movement. Those who have are always inclined to hold; always afraid to risk. No good cause in Ireland appeals for help in vain, provided those to whom it appeals are sufficiently poor. The young men who, I imagine, are volunteering to-day are for the most part poor: being poor, they will know how to save and pinch and scrape until each man of them has a rifle and a uniform. There are those among them who will give up tobacco for a spell, or at any rate reduce their consumption of tobacco; who will become total abstainers for a while; who will renounce betting; who will go less frequently to theatres, to music-halls, to picture-houses;

who will dispense with all their little luxuries and rise above all their little follies, to the sole end that they may have, each man of them, before the year is out, a Volunteer rifle on his shoulder and a Volunteer coat on his back.   Note well the companies: I prophesy that it is not the companies which draw their recruits from the most prosperous quarters that will be soonest equipped; not the sleekest-looking men that will first shoulder rifles.   When you are starting upon any noble enterprise, it is a great thing to start poor.   Wolfe Tone, reaching France with a hundred guineas in his pocket, sent three fleets against England.   James Stephens with ninety pounds in hand embarked upon the organisation of the Fenians.

In the second place, this is a movement of the people, not of the "leaders."   The leaders in Ireland have nearly always left the people at the critical moment; have sometimes sold them.   The former Volunteer movement was abandoned by its leaders; hence its ultimate failure. Grattan "led the van" of the Volunteers, but he also led the retreat of the leaders; O'Connell recoiled before the cannon at Clontarf; twice the hour of the Irish Revolution struck during Young Ireland days, and twice it struck in vain, for Meagher hesitated in Waterford, Duffy and McGee hesitated in Dublin.   Stephens refused to "give the word" in '65; he never came in '66 or '67.   I do not blame these men: you or I might have done the same.   It is a terrible responsibility to be cast upon a man, that of bidding the cannon speak and the grapeshot pour.   But in this Volunteer movement, as I understand it, the people are to be master; and it will be for the people to say when and against whom the Volunteers shall draw the sword and point the rifle.   Now, my reading of Irish history is that, however the leaders may have failed, *the instinct of the people has always been unerring.*   The Volunteers themselves, the people themselves, must keep control of this movement.   Any man or any group of men that seeks to establish an ascendancy should be dealt with summarily: such traitors to the Volunteer spirit would deserve to be shot, but it will be sufficient if they be shot *out.*

In the third place, the young men of Ireland have been to school to the Gaelic League.   Herein it seems to me lies the fact which chiefly distinguishes this generation from the other revolutionary generations of

103

the last century and a half: from the Volunteer generation of 1778, from the United Irish generation of 1798, from the Young Ireland generation of 1848, from the Fenian generation of 1867. We have known the Gaelic League, and

> "Lo, a clearness of vision has followed, lo, a purification
>   of sight."

I do not think we shall be as liable to make blunders, to pursue side issues, to mistake shadows for substance, to overlook essentials, to neglect details on the one hand or to get lost in them on the other, as were previous generations of perhaps better men. It is not merely (or at all) that we have now a theory of nationality by which to correct our instinct: indeed, I doubt if a theory of nationality be a very great gain, and plainly the instinct of the Fenian artisan was a finer thing than the soundest theory of the Gaelic League professor. It is rather that we have got into a fuller communion with what is most racy in our past: our ancestors have spoken to us anew. In a deeper sense than before we realise that Ireland is ours and that we are Ireland's. Our country wears to us a new aspect, and yet she is her most ancient self. We are as men who, having wandered long through the devious ways of a forest, see again the familiar hills and fields bathed in the light of heaven, ancient yet ever-new. And we rejoice in our hearts, and bless the goodly sun.

PEACE AND THE GAEL

(DECEMBER 1915)

When we are old (those of us who live to be old) we shall tell our grandchildren of the Christmas of 1915 as the second Christmas which saw the nations at war for the freedom of the seas; as the last Christmas, it may be, which saw Ireland, the gate of the seas, in the keeping of the English. For that is the thing for which men are bleeding to-day in France and Serbia, in Poland and Mesopotamia. The many fight to uphold a tyranny three centuries old, the most arrogant tyranny that there has ever been in the world; and the few fight to break that tyranny. Always it is the many who fight for the evil thing, and the few who fight for the good thing; and always it is the few who win. For God fights with the small battalions. If sometimes it has seemed otherwise, it is because the few who have fought for the good cause have been guilty of some secret faltering, some infidelity to their best selves, some shrinking back in the face of a tremendous duty.

The last sixteen months have been the most glorious in the history of Europe. Heroism has come back to the earth. On whichever side the men who rule the peoples have marshalled them, whether with England to uphold her tyranny of the seas, or with Germany to break that tyranny, the people themselves have gone into battle because to each the old voice that speaks out of the soil of a nation has spoken anew. Each fights for the fatherland. It is policy that moves the governments; it is patriotism that stirs the peoples. Belgium defending her soil is heroic, and so is Turkey fighting with her back to Constantinople.

It is good for the world that such things should be done. The old heart of the earth needed to be warmed with the red wine of the

105

battlefields. Such august homage was never before offered to God as this, the homage of millions of lives given gladly for love of country.

War is a terrible thing, and this is the most terrible of wars. But this war is not more terrible than the evils which it will end or help to end. It is not more terrible than the exploitation of the English masses by cruel plutocrats; it is not more terrible than the infidelity of the French masses to their old spiritual ideals; it is not more terrible than the enslavement of the Poles by Russia, than the enslavement of the Irish by England. What if the war kindles in the slow breasts of English toilers a wrath like the wrath of the French in 1789? What if the war brings France back to her altars, as sorrow brings back broken men and women to God? What if the war sets Poland and Ireland free? If the war does these things, will not the war have been worthwhile?

War is a terrible thing, but war is not an evil thing. It is the things that make war necessary that are evil. The tyrannies that wars break, the lying formulae that wars overthrow, the hypocrisies that wars strip naked, are evil. Many people in Ireland dread war because they do not know it. Ireland has not known the exhilaration of war for over a hundred years. Yet who will say that she has known the blessings of peace? When war comes to Ireland, she must welcome it as she would welcome the Angel of God. And she will.

It is because peace is so precious a boon that war is so sacred a duty. Ireland will not find Christ's peace until she has taken Christ's sword. What peace she has known in these latter days has been the devil's peace, peace with sin, peace with dishonour. It is a foul thing, dear only to men of foul breeds. Christ's peace is lovely in its coming, beautiful are its feet on the mountains. But it is heralded by terrific messengers; seraphim and cherubim blow trumpets of war before it. We must not flinch when we are passing through that uproar; we must not faint at the sight of blood. Winning through it, we (or those of us who survive) shall come unto great joy. We and our fathers have known the Pax Britannica. To our sons we must bequeath the Peace of the Gael.

GHOSTS

PREFACE

Here be ghosts that I have raised this Christmastide, ghosts of dead men that have bequeathed a trust to us living men. Ghosts are troublesome things in a house or in a family, as we knew even before Ibsen taught us. There is only one way to appease a ghost. You must do the thing it asks you. The ghosts of a nation sometimes ask very big things; and they must be appeased, whatever the cost.

Of the shade of the Norwegian dramatist I beg forgiveness for a plagiaristic, but inevitable title.

P. H. PEARSE.

ST. ENDA'S COLLEGE,
RATHFARNHAM,
Christmas Day, 1915.

GHOSTS

I

There has been nothing more terrible in Irish history than the failure of the last generation. Other generations have failed in Ireland, but they have failed nobly; or, failing ignobly, some man among them has redeemed them from infamy by the splendour of his protest. But the failure of the last generation has been mean and shameful, and no man has arisen from it to say or do a splendid thing in virtue of which it shall be forgiven. The whole episode is squalid. It will remain the one sickening chapter in a story which, gallant or sorrowful, has everywhere else some exaltation of pride.

"Is mairg do ghní go holc agus bhíos bocht ina dhiaidh," says the Irish proverb. "Woe to him that doeth evil and is poor after it." The men who have led Ireland for twenty-five years have done evil, and they are bankrupt. They are bankrupt in policy, bankrupt in credit, bankrupt now even in words. They have nothing to propose to Ireland, no way of wisdom, no counsel of courage. When they speak they speak only untruth and blasphemy. Their utterances are no longer the utterances of men. They are the mumblings and the gibberings of lost souls.

One finds oneself wondering what sin these men have been guilty of that so great a shame should come upon them. Is it that they are punished with loss of manhood because in their youth they committed a crime against manhood?.... Does the ghost of Parnell hunt them to their damnation?

Even had the men themselves been less base, their failure would have been inevitable. When one thinks over the matter for a little one sees that they have built upon an untruth. They have conceived of nationality as a material thing, whereas it is a spiritual thing. They have made the same mistake that a man would make if he were to forget that he has an immortal soul. They have not recognised in their people the

108

image and likeness of God. Hence, the nation to them is not all holy, a thing inviolate and inviolable, a thing that a man dare not sell or dishonour on pain of eternal perdition. They have thought of nationality as a thing to be negotiated about as men negotiate about a tariff or about a trade route, rather than as an immediate jewel to be preserved at all peril, a thing so sacred that it may not be brought into the market places at all or spoken of where men traffic.

He who builds on lies rears only lies. The untruth that nationality is corporeal, a thing defined by statutes and guaranteed by mutual interests, is at the base of the untruth that freedom, which is the condition of a hale nationality, is a status to be conceded rather than a glory to be achieved; and of the other untruth that it can ever be lawful in the interest of empire, in the interest of wealth, in the interest of quiet living, to forego the right to freedom. The contrary is the truth. Freedom, being a spiritual necessity, transcends all corporeal necessities, and when freedom is being considered interests should not be spoken of. Or, if the terms of the countinghouse be the ones that are best understood, let us put it that it is the highest interest of a nation to be free.

Like a divine religion, national freedom bears the marks of unity, of sanctity, of catholicity, of apostolic succession. Of unity, for it contemplates the nation as one; of sanctity, for it is holy in itself and in those who serve it; of catholicity, for it embraces all the men and women of the nation; of apostolic succession, for it, or the aspiration after it, passes down from generation to generation from the nation's fathers. A nation's fundamental idea of freedom is not affected by the accidents of time and circumstance. It does not vary with the centuries, or with the comings and goings of men or of empires. The substance of truth does not change, nor does the substance of freedom. Yesterday's definition of both the one and the other is to-day's definition and will be to-morrow's. As the body of truth which a true church teaches can neither be increased nor diminished—though truths implicit in the first definition may be made explicit in later definitions—so a true definition of freedom remains constant; it cannot be added to or subtracted from or varied in its essentials, though things implicit in it may be made explicit by a later definition. If the definition can be varied in its essentials, or added to, or subtracted from, it was not a true definition in the first instance.

To be concrete, if we to-day are fighting for something either greater than or less than the thing our fathers fought for, either our fathers did not fight for freedom at all, or we are not fighting for freedom. If I do not hold the faith of Tone, and if Tone was not a heretic, then I am. If Tone said "BREAK the connection with England," and if I say "MAINTAIN the connection with England," I may be preaching a saner (as I am certainly preaching a safer) gospel than his, but I am obviously not preaching the same gospel.

Now what Tone taught, and the fathers of our national faith before and after Tone, is ascertainable. It stands recorded. It has fulness, it has clarity, the sufficiency and the definiteness of dogma. It lives in great and memorable phrases, a grandiose national faith. They, too, have left us their Credo.

The Irish mind is the clearest mind that has ever applied itself to the consideration of nationality and of national freedom. A chance phrase of Keating's might almost stand as a definition. He spoke of Ireland as "domhan beag innti féin," a little world in herself. It was characteristic of Irish-speaking men that when they thought of the Irish nation they thought less of its outer forms and pomps than of the inner thing which was its soul. They recognised that the Irish life was the thing that mattered, and that, the Irish life dead, the Irish nation was dead. But they recognised that freedom was the essential condition of a vigorous Irish life. And for freedom they raised their ranns; for freedom they stood in battle through five bloody centuries.

II

Irish nationality is an ancient spiritual tradition, one of the oldest and most august traditions in the world. Politically, Ireland's claim has been for freedom in order to the full and perpetual life of that tradition. The generations of Ireland have gone into battle for no other thing. To the Irish mind for more than a thousand years freedom has had but one definition. It has meant not a limited freedom, a freedom conditioned by the interests of another nation, a freedom compatible with the suzerain authority of a foreign parliament, but absolute freedom, the sovereign control of Irish destinies. It has meant not the freedom of a class, but the freedom of a people. It has meant not the freedom of a geographical fragment of Ireland, but the freedom of all Ireland, of every sod of Ireland.

And the freedom thus defined has seemed to the Irish the most desirable of all earthly things. They have valued it more than land, more than wealth, more than ease, more than empire.

"Fearr bheith i mbarraibh fuairbheann
I bhfeitheamh shuainghearr ghrinnmhear,
Ag seilg troda ar fhéinn eachtrann
'Gá bhfuil fearann bhur sinnsear,"

said Angus Mac Daighre O'Daly. "Better to be on the tops of the old bens keeping watch, short of sleep yet gladsome, urging fight against the foreign soldiery that hold your fathers' land." And Fearflatha O'Gnive spoke for the generations that preferred exile to slavery:

"Má thug an deonughadh dhi
Sacsa nua darbh' ainm Eire
Bheith re a linn-si i láimh bíodhbhadh,
Do'n inse is cáir ceileabhradh."

"If thou hast consented (O God) that there be a new England named Ireland, to be ever in the grip of a foe then to this isle we must bid farewell."

I make the contention that the national demand of Ireland is fixed and determined; that that demand has been made by every generation; that we of this generation receive it as a trust from our fathers; that we are bound by it; that we have not the right to alter it or to abate it by one jot or tittle; and that any undertaking made in the name of Ireland to accept in full satisfaction of Ireland's claim anything less than the generations of Ireland have stood for is null and void, binding on Ireland neither by the law of God nor by the law of nations.

A nation can bind itself by treaty to do or to forego specific things, as a man can bind himself by contract; but no treaty which places a nation's body and soul in the power of another nation, no treaty which abnegates a nation's nationhood, is binding on that nation, any more than a contract of perpetual slavery is binding on an individual. If in a drunken frolic or in mere abject unmanliness I sell myself and my posterity to a slaveholder to have and to hold as a chattel property to himself and his heirs, am I bound by the contract? Are my children bound by it? Can any legal contract make a wrong thing binding? And if not, can a contract executed in my name, but without my express or implied authority, make a wrong thing binding on me and on my children's children?

Ireland's historic claim is for Separation. Ireland has authorised no man to abate that claim. The man who, in the name of Ireland, accepts as "a final settlement" anything less by one fraction of an iota than Separation from England will be repudiated by the new generation as surely as O'Connell was repudiated by the generation that came after him. The man who, in return for the promise of a thing which is not merely less than Separation, but which denies Separation and proclaims the Union perpetual, the man who, in return for this, declares peace between Ireland and England and sacrifices to England as a peace-holocaust the blood of fifty thousand Irishmen, is guilty of so immense an infidelity, so immense a crime against the Irish nation, that one can only say of him that it were better for that man (as it were certainly better for his country) that he had not been born.

I have proved this terrible infidelity against a living Irishman, against all who have supported him, against the majority of Irishmen who are now past middle life, if I can establish that the historic claim of Ireland has been for Separation. And I proceed to establish this.

III

It will be conceded to me that the Irish who opposed the landing of the English in 1169 were Separatists. Else why oppose those who came to annex? It will be conceded that the twelve generations of the Irish nation, the "mere Irish" of the English state-papers, who maintained a winning fight against English domination in Ireland from 1169 to 1509 (roughly speaking), were Separatist generations. The Irish princes who brought over Edward Bruce and made him King of Ireland were plainly Separatists. The Mac Murrough who hammered the English for fifty years and twice out-generaled and out-fought an English king was obviously a Separatist. The turbulence of Shane O'Neill becomes understandable when it is realised that he was a Separatist; Separatists are apt, from of old, to be cranky and sore-headed. The Fitzmaurice who brought the Spaniards to Smerwick Harbour was a mere Separatist: he was one of the pro-Spaniards of those days—Separatists are always pro-Something of which the English disapprove. That proud dissembling O'Neill and that fiery O'Donnell who banded the Irish and the Anglo-Irish against the English, who brought the Spaniards to Kinsale, who fought the war that, but for a guide losing his way, would have been known as the Irish War of Separation, were, it will be granted, Separatists. Rory O'More was uncommonly like a Separatist. Owen Roe O'Neill was admittedly a Separatist, the leader of the Separatist Party in the Confederation of Kilkenny. When O'Neill sent his veterans into the battle-gap at Benburb with the words "In the name of the Father, Son, and Holy Ghost, charge for Ireland!" the word "Ireland" had for him a very definite meaning. If Sarsfield fought technically for an English king, the popular literature of the day leaves no doubt that in the people's mind he stood for Separation, and that it was not an English faction but the Irish nation that rallied behind the walls of Limerick. So, up to 1691 Ireland was Separatist.

IV

During the first three-quarters of the eighteenth century a miracle wrought itself. So does the germ of Separation inhere in the soil of Ireland that the very Cromwellians and Williamites were infected with it. The Palesmen began to realise themselves as part of the Irish nation, and in the fulness of time they declared themselves Separatists. While this process was slowly accomplishing itself, the authentic voice of Ireland is to be sought in her literature. And that literature is a Separatist literature. The "secret songs" of the dispossessed Irish are the most fiercely Separatist utterances in any literature. Not until Mitchel did Anglo-Irish literature catch up that Irish vehemence. The poet of the "Roman Vision" sang of the Ireland that was to be:

> "No man shall be bound unto England
> Nor hold friendship with dour Scotsmen,
> There shall be no place in Ireland for outlanders,
> Nor any recognition for the English speech."

The prophetic voice of Mitchel seems to ring in this:

> "The world hath conquered, the wind hath scattered like
>   dust
> Alexander, Caesar, and all that shared their sway,
> Tara is grass, and behold how Troy lieth low, —
> And even the English, perchance their hour will come!"

An unknown poet, seeing the corpse of an Englishman hanging on a tree, sings:

> "Good is thy fruit, O tree!
> The luck of thy fruit on every bough!
> Would that the trees of Inisfail
> Were full of thy fruit every day!"

The poet of the "Druimfhionn Donn Dílis" cries:

"The English I'd rend as I'd rend an old brogue,
And that's how I'd win me the Druimfhionn Donn Og!"

I do not defend this blood-thirstiness any more than I apologise for it. I simply point it out as the note of a literature.

Finally, when the poet of the "Róisín Dubh" declares that

"The Erne shall rise in rude torrents, hills shall be rent,
The sea shall roll in red waves, and blood be poured out,
Every mountain glen in Ireland, and the bogs shall quake,"

is it to be supposed that these apocalyptic disturbances are to usher in merely a statutory legislation subordinate to the imperial parliament at Westminster whose supreme authority over Ireland shall remain unimpaired "anything in this Act notwithstanding?"

The student of Irish affairs who does not know Irish literature is ignorant of the awful intensity of the Irish desire for Separation as he is ignorant of one of the chief forces which make Separation inevitable.

V

The first man who spoke, or seemed to speak, for Ireland and who was not a Separatist was Henry Grattan. And it was against Henry Grattan's Constitution that Wolfe Tone and the United Irishmen rose. Thus the Pale made common cause with the Gael and declared itself Separatist. It will be conceded that Wolfe Tone was a Separatist: he is *The* Separatist. It will be conceded that Robert Emmet was a Separatist. O'Connell was not a Separatist: but, as the United Irishmen revolted against Grattan, Young Ireland revolted against O'Connell. And Young Ireland, in its final development, was Separatist. To Young Ireland belong three of the great Separatist voices. After Young Ireland the

Fenians; and it will be admitted that the Fenians were Separatists. They guarded themselves against future misrepresentation by calling themselves the Irish Republican Brotherhood.

It thus appears that Ireland has been Separatist up to the beginning of the generation that is now growing old. Separatism, in fact, is the national position. Whenever an Irish leader has taken up a position different from the national position he has been repudiated by the next generation. The United Irishmen repudiated Grattan. The Young Irelanders repudiated O'Connell. The Irish Volunteers have repudiated Mr. Redmond.

The chain of the Separatist tradition has never once snapped during the centuries. Veterans of Kinsale were in the '41; veterans of Benburb followed Sarsfield. The poets kept the fires of the nation burning from Limerick to Dungannon. Napper Tandy of the Volunteers was Napper Tandy of the United Irishmen. The Russell of 1803 was the Russell of 1798. The Robert Holmes of '98 and 1803 lived to be a Young Irelander. Three Young Irelanders were the founders of Fenianism. The veterans of Fenianism stand to-day with the Irish Volunteers. So the end of the Separatist tradition is not yet.

VI

It would be very instructive to examine in its breadth and depth, in its connotations as well as in its denotations, the Irish definition of freedom; and I propose to do this in a sequel to the present essay. For my immediate purpose it is sufficient to state that definition merely as a principle involving essentially the idea of Independence, Separation, a distinct and unfettered national existence.

The conception of an Irish nation has been developed in modern times chiefly by four great minds. On a little reflection one comes to see that what has been contributed by other minds has been almost entirely by way of explanation and illustration of what has been laid down by the four master minds; that the four have been the Fathers, and that the others are just their commentarists. Accordingly, when I have named the four names, there will be hardly any need to name any other names. Indeed, it will be difficult to think of names that can be named in the same breath with these, difficult to think of men who have reached anything like the same stature or who have stretched out even half as far.

The names are those of Theobald Wolfe Tone, Thomas Davis, James Fintan Lalor, and John Mitchel.

It is a question here of political teachers, not of mere political leaders. O'Connell was a more effective political leader than either Lalor or Mitchel, but no one gives O'Connell a place in the history of political thought. He did not propound, he did not even attempt to propound, any body of political truths. He was a political strategist of extraordinary ability, a rhetorician of almost superhuman power. But we owe no political doctrine to O'Connell except the obviously untrue doctrine that liberty is too dearly purchased at the price of a single drop of blood. The political position of O'Connell—his falling back on the treaty of 1782-3—was not the statement of any national principle, the embodiment of any political truth—it was an able, though as it happened unsuccessful, strategical move.

Parnell must be considered. If one had to add a fifth to the four I have named, the fifth would inevitably be Parnell. Now, Parnell was less a political thinker than an embodied conviction; a flame that seared, a sword that stabbed. He deliberately disclaimed political theories, deliberately confined himself to political action. He did the thing that lay nearest to his hand, struck at the English with such weapons as were available. His instinct was a Separatist instinct; and, far from being prepared to accept Home Rule as a "final settlement between the two nations," he was always careful to make it clear that, whether Home Rule came or did not come, the way must be left open for the achievement of the greater thing. In 1885 he said:

"It is given to none of us to forecast the future, and just as it is impossible for us to say in what way or by what means the national question may be settled—in what way full justice may be done to Ireland—so it is impossible for us to say to what extent that justice should be done. We cannot ask for less than the restitution of Grattan's

Parliament, with its important privileges and wide and far-reaching constitution. We cannot, under the British constitution, ask for more than the restitution of Grattan's Parliament, but no man has a right to fix the boundary of the march of a nation. No man has a right to say 'Thus far shalt thou go, and no further;' and we have never attempted to fix the *ne plus ultra* to the progress of Ireland's nationhood, and we never shall. But, gentlemen, while we leave these things to time, circumstances, and the future, we must each one of us resolve in our own hearts that we shall at all times do everything that within us lies to obtain for Ireland the fullest measure of her rights. In this way we shall avoid difficulties and contentions amongst each other. In this way we shall not give up anything which the future may put in favour of our country; and while we struggle to-day for that which may seem possible for us without combination, we must struggle for it with the proud consciousness that we shall not do anything to hinder or prevent better men who may come after us from gaining better things than those for which we now contend."

And again, in the same year:

"Ireland a nation! Ireland has been a nation: she is a nation; and she shall be a nation.... England will respect you in proportion as you and we respect ourselves. They will not give anything to Ireland out of justice or righteousness. They will concede you your liberties and your rights when they must and no sooner.... We can none of us do more than strive for that which may seem attainable to-day; but we ought at the same time to recollect that we should not impede or hamper the march of our nation; and although our programme may be limited and small, it should be such a one as shall not prevent hereafter the fullest realisation of the hopes of Ireland; and we shall, at least if we keep this principle in mind, have this consolation that, while we may have done something to enable Ireland in some measure to retain her position as a nation, to strengthen her position as a nation, we shall have done nothing to hinder others who may come after us from taking up the work with perhaps greater strength, ability, power, and advantages than we possess, and from pushing to that glorious and happy conclusion which is embodied in the words of the toast which I now ask you to drink—'Ireland a nation!'"

These words justify me in summoning the pale and angry ghost of Parnell to stand beside the ghosts of Tone and Davis and Lalor and Mitchel. If words mean anything, these mean that to Parnell the final and inevitable and infinitely desirable goal of Ireland was Separation; and that those who thought it prudent and feasible, as he did, to proceed to Separation by Home Rule must above all things do nothing that might impair the Separatist position or render the future task of the Separatists more difficult. Of Parnell it may be said with absolute truth that he never surrendered the national position. His successors have surrendered it. They have written on his monument in Dublin those noble words of his, that no man has a right to fix the boundary of the march of a nation; and then they have accepted the Home Rule Act as a "final settlement" between Ireland and England. It is as if a man were to write on a monument "I believe in God and in Life Everlasting" and then to sell his chance of Heaven to the Evil One for a purse, not of gold, but of I.O.U.'s.

If I could think of any other name that, with due regard for proportion, could be named with the great names, I should name it and proceed to examine its claims. But I can think of no other name. I can think of heroic leaders like Emmet; I can think of brilliant rhetoricians like Meagher; I can think of able and powerful publicists like Duffy; I can think of secret organisers like Stephens: and all these were Separatist. But I cannot think of anyone who has left behind him a *body of teaching* that requires to be examined. Emmet's mind was as great as any of the four minds except Tone's, but we have not its fruits; only an indication of its riches in his speech from the dock, and of its strength and sanity in the draft proclamation for his Provisional Government.

I can think, again, of three great political thinkers of Anglo-Ireland before Tone: Berkeley, Swift, and Burke. And from the writings of these three I could construct the case for Irish Separatism. But this would be irrelevent to my purpose. I am seeking to find, not those who have thought most wisely about Ireland, but those who have thought most authentically for Ireland, the voices that have come out of the Irish struggle itself. And those voices, subject to what I have said as to Parnell, are the voices of Tone, of Davis, of Lalor, of Mitchel. Let us see what they have said.

VII

First, Tone. Of 1790:

"I made speedily what was to me a great discovery, though I might have found it in Swift and Molyneux, that the influence of England was the radical vice of our Government, and consequently that Ireland would never be either free, prosperous, or happy until she was independent, and that independence was unattainable whilst the connection with England lasted."

Of 1791:

"It [a communication from Russell] immediately set me thinking more seriously than I had yet done upon the state of Ireland. I soon formed my theory, and on that theory I have invariably acted ever since.

"To subvert the tyranny of our execrable Government, to break the connection with England, the never-failing source of all our political evils, and to assert the independence of my country—these were my objects. To unite the whole people of Ireland, to abolish the memory of all past dissensions, and to substitute the common name of Irishman in the place of the denominations of Protestant, Catholic, and Dissenter— these were my means."

I hold all Irish nationalism to be implicit in these words. Davis was to make explicit certain things here implicit, Lalor certain other things; Mitchel was to thunder the whole in words of apocalyptic wrath and splendour. But the Credo is here: "I believe in One Irish Nation and that Free."

And before his judges Tone thus testified:

"I mean not to give you the trouble of bringing judicial proof to convict me, legally, of having acted in hostility to the Government of his Britannic Majesty in Ireland. I admit the fact. From my earliest youth I have regarded the connection between Ireland and Great Britain as the curse of the Irish nation, and felt convinced that, while it lasted, this country could never be free nor happy. My mind has been confirmed in this opinion by the experience of every succeeding year, and the conclusions which I have drawn from every fact before my eyes. In consequence, I determined to apply all the powers which my individual efforts could move in order to separate the two countries."

Next, Davis:

"...Will she [England] allow us, for good or ill, to govern ourselves, and see if we cannot redress our own griefs. 'No, never, never,' she says, 'though all Ireland cried for it—never! Her fields shall be manured with the shattered limbs of her sons, and her hearths quenched in their blood; but never, while England has a ship or a soldier, shall Ireland be free.'

"And this is your answer? We shall see—we shall see!

"And now, Englishmen, listen to us! Though you were to-morrow to give us the best tenures on earth—though you were to equalise Presbyterian, Catholic, and Episcopalian —though you were to give us the amplest representation in your Senate—though you were to restore our absentees, disencumber us of your debt, and redress every one of our fiscal wrongs—and though, in addition to all this, you plundered the treasuries of the world to lay gold at our feet, and exhausted the resources of your genius to do us worship and honour—still we tell you—we tell you, in the names of liberty and country—we tell you, in the name of enthusiastic hearts, thoughtful souls, and fearless spirits—we tell you, by the past, the present, and the future, we would spurn your gifts, if the condition were that Ireland should remain a province. We tell you, and all whom it may concern, come what may—bribery or deceit, justice, policy, or war—we tell you, in the name of Ireland, that Ireland shall be a Nation!"

Lest it may be pretended (as it has been pretended) that the nationhood thus claimed in the name of Ireland by this passionate nationalist was a mere statutory "nationhood," federalism or something less, I quote a passage which makes it clear that Davis (loyally though he supported the official policy of the *Nation*, which at that stage did not go beyond Repeal) was thinking all the time of a sovereign independent Ireland. Urging the need of foreign alliances for Ireland, he writes (the italics are Davis's):

"When Ireland is a nation she will not, with her vast population[12] and her military character, require such alliances as a *security* against an English *re-conquest*; but they will be useful in banishing any *dreams of invasion* which might *otherwise* haunt the brain of our old enemy."

Elsewhere Davis sums up the national position in a sentence worthy of Tone:

"Ireland's aspiration is for unbounded nationality."

Next, Lalor:

"Repeal, in its vulgar meaning, I look on as utterly impracticable by any mode of action whatever; and the constitution of '82 was absurd, worthless, and worse than worthless. The English Government will never concede or surrender to any species of moral force whatsoever; and the country-peasantry will never arm and fight for it—neither will I. If I am to stake life and fame it must assuredly be for something better and greater, more likely to last, more likely to succeed, and better worth success. And a stronger passion, a higher purpose, a nobler and more needful enterprise is fermenting in the hearts of the people. A mightier question moves Ireland to-day than that of merely repealing the Act of

---

[12] Nearly 9,000,000 then.

Union. Not the constitution that Wolfe Tone died to abolish, but the constitution that Tone died to obtain—independence; full and absolute independence for this island, and for every man within this island. Into no movement that would leave an enemy's garrison in possession of all our lands, masters of our liberties, our lives, and all our means of life and happiness—into no such movement will a single man of the greycoats enter with an armed hand, whatever the town population may do. On a wider fighting field, with stronger positions and greater resources than are afforded by the paltry question of Repeal, must we close for our final struggle with England, or sink
and surrender.

"Ireland her own—Ireland her own, and all therein, from the sod to the sky. The soil of Ireland for the people of Ireland, to have and hold from God alone who gave it—to have and to hold to them and to their heirs for ever, without suit or service, faith or fealty, rent or render, to any power under Heaven."

And again:

"Not to repeal the Union, then, but the conquest—not to disturb or dismantle the Empire, but to abolish it utterly for ever—not to fall back on '82, but to act up to '48—not to resume or restore an old constitution, but to found a new nation and raise up a free people, and strong as well as free, and secure as well as strong, based on a peasantry rooted like rocks in the soil of the land—this is my object, as I hope it is yours; and this, you may be assured, is the easier as it is the nobler and more pressing enterprise."

And yet again:

"In the case of Ireland now there is but *one fact* to deal with, and *one question* to be considered. The *fact* is this—that there are at present in occupation of our country some 40,000 armed men, in the livery and service of England; and the *question* is—how best and soonest to kill and capture those 40,000 men."

Lastly Mitchel takes up his hymn of hate against the Empire:

"*The Ego*—And do you read Ireland's mind in the canting of O'Connell's son? or in the sullen silence of a gagged and disarmed people? Tell me not of O'Connell's son. His father begat him in moral force, and in patience and perseverance did his mother conceive him. I swear to you there are blood and brain in Ireland yet, as the world one day shall know. God! let me live to see it. On that great day of the Lord, when the kindreds and tongues and nations of the old earth shall give their banners to the wind, let this poor carcase have but breath and strength enough to stand under Ireland's immortal Green!

"*Doppelganger*—Do you allude to the battle of Armageddon? I know you have been reading the Old Testament of late.

"*The Ego*—Yes. 'Who is this that cometh from Edom; with dyed garments from Bozrah? This that is glorious in his apparel travelling in the garments of his strength? Wherefore art thou red in thine apparel, and thy garments like him that treadeth in the wine vat? I have trodden the wine press alone, and of the people there was none with me: for I will tread them in mine anger and trample them in my fury, and their blood shall be sprinkled upon my garments, and I will stain all my raiment. For the day of vengeance is in my heart.' Also an aspiration of King David haunts my memory when I think on Ireland and her wrongs: '*That thy foot may be dipped in the blood of thine enemies, and that the tongue of thy dogs may be red through the same.*'"

Thus Tone, thus Davis, thus Lalor, thus Mitchel, thus Parnell. Methinks I have raised some ghosts that will take a little laying.

THE SEPARATIST IDEA

PREFACE

This is the first of three pamphlets in which I propose to develop the contention put forward in "Ghosts," the whole forming a continuous argument. The further pamphlets of the series will be entitled "The Spiritual Nation" and "The Sovereign People," respectively.

P. H. PEARSE.

ST. ENDA'S COLLEGE,
RATHFARNHAM,
1st February, 1916.

THE SEPARATIST IDEA

I

In stating a little while ago the Irish definition of freedom, I said that it would be well worth while to examine that definition in its breadth and depth, in its connotations as well as in its denotations, contenting myself for the moment with making clear its essential idea of Independence, Separation, a distinct and unfettered national existence. And I said that I proposed to do this in a sequel. Such a sequel is necessary, for, while the statement that national freedom means a distinct and unfettered national existence is a true and complete statement of the nature of national freedom, it is not a sufficient revelation of the minds that have developed the conception of freedom among us Irish, not sufficiently quick with their thought nor sufficiently passionate with their desire. Freedom is so splendid a thing that one cannot worthily state it in the terms of a definition; one has to write it in some flaming symbol or to sing it in music riotous with the uproar of heaven. A Danton and a Mitchel can speak more adequately of freedom than a Voltaire and a Burke, for they have drunk more deeply of that wine with which God inebriates the votaries of vision. But even the sublimest things, the Trinity and the Incarnation, can be stated in terms of philosophy, and it is needful to do this now and then, though such a statement in no wise affects the spiritual fact which one either feels or does not feel. So, it is sometimes necessary to state what nationality is, what freedom, though one's statement may not reveal the awful beauty of his nation's soul to a single man or move a single village to put up its barricade.

The purpose, then, of such statements? At least they define the truth, and enable men to see who holds the truth and who hugs the falsehood. For there is an absolute truth in such matters, and the truth is ascertainable. The truth is old, and it has been handed down to us by our fathers. It is not a new thing, devised to meet the exigencies of a situation. That is the definition of an expedient.

Now, the truth as to what a nation's nationality is, what a nation's freedom, is not to be found in the statute-book of the nation's enemy. It is to be found in the books of the nation's fathers.

II

I have named Tone and Davis and Lalor and Mitchel as the four among us moderns who have chiefly developed the conception of an Irish nation. Others, I have said, have for the most part only interpreted and illustrated what has been taught by these; these are the Fathers and the rest are just their commentarists. And I need not repeat here my reasons for naming no other with these unless the other be Parnell, whom I name tentatively as the man who saw most deeply and who spoke most splendidly for the Irish nation since the great seers and speakers. I go on to examine what these have taught of Irish freedom. And first as to Tone. He stands first in point of time, and first in point of greatness. Indeed, he is, as I believe, the greatest man of our nation; the greatest-hearted and the greatest-minded.

We have to consider here Tone the thinker rather than Tone the man of action. The greatest of our men of action since Hugh O'Neill, he is the greatest of all our political thinkers. His greatness, both as a man and as a thinker, consists in his sheer reality. There is no froth of rhetoric, no dilution of sentimentality in Tone; he has none even of the noble oratoric quality of a Mitchel. A man of extraordinarily deep emotion, he nevertheless thought with relentless logic, and his expression in exposition or argument is always the due and inevitable garb of his thought. He was a great visionary; but, like all the great visionaries, he had a firm grip upon realities, he was fundamentally sane.

It is necessary at times to insist on Tone's intellectual austerity, because the man's humanity was so gracious that his human side constantly overshadows, for us as for his contemporaries, his grave intellectual side. Most men of his greatness are loved at best by a few, feared or disliked or mistrusted by the many. Tone was one of the extremely rare great men whose greatness is crowned by those gifts of humility and sweetness that compel affection. Some men are misunderstood because they are disliked; a few men are in danger of being misunderstood because they are loved. If the greatest thing in Tone was his heroic soul, the soul that was gay in death and defeat, the second greatest thing was his austere and piercing intellect. That intellect has dominated Irish political thought for over a century. It has given us our political definitions and values. Constantly we refer doctrines and leaders and policies to its standards, measuring them by the mind of Tone as an American measures men and policies by the minds that shaped the Declaration of Independence. Tone's mind was in a very true sense a revolutionary mind. The spokesmen of the French Revolution itself did not base things more fundamentally on essential right and justice than Tone did, did not pierce through outer strata to a firmer bedrock than he found. And it was an original mind. Influenced no doubt by contemporary minds, and responsive to every thought-wave that vibrated in either hemisphere, Tone for the most part worked out his own political system in his own way. He did not inherit or merely accept his principles; he thought himself into them.

Tone's first political utterance was a pamphlet in defence of the Whig Club, entitled "A Review of the last Session of Parliament" (1790). Of this pamphlet he writes in his Autobiography:

"…Though I was very far from entirely approving the system of the Whig Club, and much less their principles and motives, yet, seeing them at the time the best constituted political body which the country afforded, and agreeing with most of their positions, though my own private opinions went infinitely farther, I thought I could venture on their defence without violating my consistency. "

The pamphlet contains no definitely Separatist teaching. Before the end of the year, however, Tone had found his voice. It is a Separatist that speaks in "The Spanish War" (1790), but a cautious Separatist, one who is feeling his way. Tone himself describes the expansion of his views which had taken place between the publication of his first and his second pamphlets:

"A closer examination into the history of my native country had very considerably extended my views, and, as I was sincerely and honestly attached to her interests, I soon found reason not to regret that the Whigs had not thought me an object worthy of their cultivation. I made speedily what was to me a great discovery, though I might have found it in Swift and Molyneux, that the influence of England was the radical vice of our Government, and consequently that Ireland would never be either free, prosperous, or happy until she was independent, and that independence was unattainable whilst the connection with England existed."

Accordingly:

"On the appearance of a rupture with Spain, I wrote a pamphlet to prove that Ireland was not bound by the declaration of war, but might, and ought, as an independent nation, to stipulate for a neutrality. In examining this question, I advanced the question of separation, with scarcely any reserve, much less disguise; but the public mind was by no means so far advanced as I was, and my pamphlet made not the slightest impression."

The pamphlet, in fact, tended to prove the impossibility of Grattan's constitution, *i.e.*, of the co-existence of a British connection with a sovereign Irish Parliament. It did not propound this in so many words, but the logical conclusion from its extraordinarily able and subtle argument is that no "half-way house" is possible as a permanent solution of the issue between Ireland and England. There were and are only two alternatives: an enslaved Ireland and a free Ireland. A "dual monarchy" is, in the nature of things, only a temporary expedient.

In 1790 Tone met Thomas Russell. Theirs was the most memorable of Irish friendships. It was in conversations and correspondence with Russell that Tone's political ideas reached their maturity. When he next speaks it is with plenary meaning and clear definition. Towards the end of 1790 he made his first attempt in political organisation. He founded a club of seven or eight members "eminent for their talents and patriotism and who had already more or less distinguished themselves by their literary productions." It was a failure, and the failure satisfied Tone that "men of genius, to be of use, must not be collected in numbers." In 1791 Russell went to Belfast. An attempt of Russell's to induce the Belfast Volunteers to adopt a declaration in favour of Catholic emancipation, which Tone had prepared at his request, was unsuccessful. Russell wrote to Tone an account of the discussion, and, says Tone:

"It immediately set me thinking more seriously than I had yet done upon the state of Ireland. I soon formed my theory, and on that theory I have invariably acted ever since.

"To subvert the tyranny of our execrable Government, to break the connection with England, the never-failing source of all our political evils, and to assert the independence of my country—these were my objects. To unite the whole people of Ireland, to abolish the memory of all past dissensions, and to substitute the common name of Irishman in place of the denominations of Protestant, Catholic, and Dissenter—these were my means."

I have said that I hold all Irish nationalism to be implicit in these words. Davis was to make explicit certain things here implicit, Lalor certain other things. But the Credo is here: "I believe in One Irish Nation and that Free."

Tone had convinced himself as to the end and the means. And now for work:

"I sat down accordingly, and wrote a pamphlet addressed to the Dissenters, and which I entitled 'An Argument on behalf of the Catholics of Ireland,' the object of which was to convince them that they and the Catholics had but one common interest and one common enemy; that the depression and slavery of Ireland was produced and perpetuated by the divisions existing between them, and that, consequently, to assert the independence of their country, and their own individual liberties, it was necessary to forget all former feuds, to consolidate the entire strength of the whole nation, and to form for the future but one people."

This pamphlet, signed "A Northern Whig," gave Tone his place in Irish politics. The Catholic leaders approached him and commenced the connection which led ultimately to his selection as their agent; the Volunteers of Belfast elected him an honorary member of their corps. He was soon afterwards invited to Belfast, where he founded, with Russell, Neilson, the Simmses, Sinclair, and MacCabe, the first club of United Irishmen. Tone wrote for the United Irishmen the following declaration:

"In the present great era of reform when unjust governments are falling in every quarter of Europe; when religious persecution is compelled to abjure her tyranny over conscience; when the Rights of Man are ascertained in Theory and that Theory substantiated by Practice; when antiquity can no longer defend absurd and oppressive forms against the common sense and common interests of mankind; when all government is acknowledged to originate from the people, and to be so far only obligatory as it protects their rights and promotes their welfare; we think it our duty as Irishmen to come forward and state what we feel to be our heavy grievance, and what we know to be its effectual remedy.

"We have no National Government; we are ruled by Englishmen and the servants of Englishmen, whose object is the interest of another country; whose instrument is corruption; whose strength is the weakness of Ireland; and these men have the whole of the power and patronage of the country as means to seduce and subdue the honesty and the spirit of her representatives in the legislature. Such an extrinsic power, acting with uniform force in a direction too frequently opposite to the true line of our obvious interests, can be resisted with effect solely by unanimity, decision, and spirit in the people, qualities which may be exerted most legally, constitutionally, and efficaciously by that great measure essential to the prosperity and freedom of Ireland—an equal Representation of all the People in Parliament...."

The declaration was not openly Separatist. Tone, however, avows that, while not yet definitely a republican, his ultimate goal even as early as 1791 was Separation: the union of Irishmen was to be but a means to an end. Commenting on the foundation (9th November, 1791) of the Dublin Club of United Irishmen, in which the republican Tandy co-operated with him, Tone writes:

"For my own part, I think it right to mention that, at this time the establishment of a Republic was not the immediate object of my speculations. My object was to secure the independence of my country under any form of government, to which I was led by a hatred of England so deeply rooted in my nature that it was rather an instinct than a principle. I left to others, better qualified for the inquiry, the investigation and merits of the different forms of government, and I contented myself with labouring on my own system, which was luckily in perfect coincidence as to its operation with that of those men who viewed the question on a broader and juster scale than I did at the time I mention."

Thus, Tone in November 1791 had not yet settled his views on abstract theories of government, but on the practical business of separating Ireland from England his resolve was fixed and unshakable.

In June 1791 there had been issued a secret Manifesto to the Friends of Freedom in Ireland which is attributed to Tone in collaboration with Neilson and others. Tone himself makes no reference to this document in his Autobiography. If it is really his it is the nearest approach to a formulation of the theory of freedom which we have from the mind of this essentially practical statesman. Whether it be Tone's or another's, it is one of the noblest utterances of the age and it is a document of primary importance in the history of Ireland. It may be described as the first manifesto of modern Irish democracy. It bases the Irish claim to freedom on the bedrock foundation of human rights:

"This society is likely to be a means the most powerful for the promotion of a great end. What end? The Rights of Man in Ireland. The greatest happiness of the greatest numbers in this island, the inherent and indefeasible claims of every free nation to rest in this nation—the will and the power to be happy, to pursue the common weal as an individual pursues his private welfare, and to stand in insulated independence, an imperatorial people.

"The greatest happiness of the Greatest Number. On the rock of this principle let this society rest; by this let it judge and determine every political question, and whatever is necessary for this end let it not be accounted hazardous, but rather our interest, our duty, our glory, and our common religion: The Rights of Man are the Rights of God, and to vindicate the one is to maintain the other. We must be free in order to serve Him whose service is perfect freedom....

"'Dieu et mon Droit' (God and my right) is the motto of kings. 'Dieu et la liberté' (God and liberty), exclaimed Voltaire when he beheld Franklin, his fellow-citizen of the world. 'Dieu et nos Droits ' (God and our rights) —let every Irishman cry aloud to each other the cry of mercy, of justice, and of victory."

The Rights of Man in Ireland is almost an adequate definition of Irish freedom. And the historic claim of Ireland has never been more worthily stated than in these words: "*The inherent and indefeasible claims of every free nation to rest in this nation—the will and the power to be happy, to pursue the common weal as an individual pursues his private welfare, and to stand in insulated independence, an imperatorial people.*"

The deep and radical nature of Tone's revolutionary work, the subtlety and power of the man himself, cannot be grasped unless it is clearly remembered that this is the secret manifesto of the movement of which the carefully constitutional declaration of the United Irishmen is the public manifesto. Tone himself, in a letter to Russell at the beginning of 1792, admits his ulterior designs while at the same time laying stress on the necessity of caution in public utterances. Referring to the declaration of the United Irishmen, he says:

"The foregoing contains my true and sincere opinion of the state of this country, *so far as in the present juncture it may be advisable to publish it.* They certainly fall short of the truth, but truth itself must sometimes condescend to temporise. My unalterable opinion is that the bane of Irish prosperity is in the influence of England: I believe that influence will ever be extended while the connection between the countries continues; nevertheless, as I know that opinion is, *for the present*, too hardy, though a very little time may establish it universally, I have not made it a part of the resolutions, I have only proposed to set up a reformed parliament, as a barrier against that mischief which every honest man that will open his eyes must see in every instance overbears the interest of Ireland: I have not said one word that looks like a wish for *separation*, though I give it to you and your friends as my most decided opinion that such an event would be a regeneration to this country."

In 1792 Tone became agent to the General Committee of the Catholics. Before the end of the year his dream of a union between the Catholics and the Dissenters was an accomplished fact. In December the Catholic Convention met. Catching Tone's spirit, it demanded complete emancipation. The Government proposed a compromise to the leaders. Tone was against any compromise, but the Catholic leaders yielded. "Merchants, I see, make bad revolutionists," commented Tone. The Act of 1793, admitting Catholics to the Parliamentary franchise, marks the end of Tone's "constitutional" period. He pressed on towards Separation, adopting revolutionary methods. The United Irishmen were reorganised as a secret association, with "a Republican Government and Separation from England" as its aims. In 1795 Tone, compromised by his relations with Jackson, left Ireland for America. It was out of settled policy that at this stage he chose exile rather than a contest with the Government. He had already conceived the idea of appealing for help to the French Republic. Shortly before he left Dublin he went out with Russell to Rathfarnham, to see Thomas Addis Emmet.

"As we walked together into town I opened my plan to them both. I told them that I considered my compromise with Government to extend no further than the banks of the Delaware, and that the moment I landed

I was free to follow any plan which might suggest itself to me, for the emancipation of my country.... I then proceeded to tell them that my intention was, immediately on my arrival in Philadelphia, to wait on the French Minister, to detail to him, fully, the situation of affairs in Ireland, to endeavour to obtain a recommendation to the French Government, and, if I succeeded so far, to leave my family in America, and to set off instantly for Paris, and apply, in the name of my country, for the assistance of France to enable us to assert our independence."

To the fulfilment of this purpose Tone devoted the three years of life that remained to him. He landed in France in 1796. The notes in his Journal of his conferences with the representatives of the French Government and the two masterly memorials which he submitted to the Executive Directory remain the fullest and most practical statement, not only of the necessity of Separation, but of the means by which Separation is to be attained, that has been made by any Irishman. In the concluding passage of his second memorial Tone sums up as follows:

"I submit to the wisdom of the French Government that England is the implacable, inveterate, irreconcilable enemy of the Republic, which never can be in perfect security while that nation retains the dominion of the sea; that, in consequence, every possible effort should be made to humble her pride and to reduce her power; that it is in Ireland, *and in Ireland only*, that she is vulnerable—a fact of the truth of which the French Government cannot be too strongly impressed; that by establishing a free Republic in Ireland they attach to France a grateful ally whose cordial assistance, in peace and war, she might command, and who, from situation and produce, could most essentially serve her: that at the same time they cut off from England her most firm support, in losing which she is laid under insuperable difficulties in recruiting her army, and especially in equipping, victualling, and manning her navy, which, unless for the resources she drew from Ireland, she would be absolutely unable to do; that by these means and, suffer me to add, *by these means only*—her arrogance can be effectually humbled, and her enormous and increasing power at sea reduced within due bounds—an object essential, not only to France, but to all Europe; that it is at least possible, by the measures mentioned, that not only her future resources, as to her navy, may be intercepted and cut off at the fountain head, but that a part of her fleet may be actually transferred to the Republic of Ireland; that the Irish people are united and prepared, and want but the means to begin: that, not to speak of the policy or the pleasure of revenge in humbling a haughty and implacable rival, it is in itself a great and splendid act of generosity, worthy of the Republic, to rescue a whole nation from a slavery under which they have groaned for six hundred years; that it is for the glory of France, after emancipating Holland and receiving Belgium into her bosom, to establish one more free Republic in Europe; that it is for her interest to cut off for ever, as she now may do, one-half of the resources of England, and lay her under extreme difficulties in the employment of the other. For all these reasons, in the name of justice, of humanity, of freedom, of my own country, and of France herself, I supplicate the Directory to take into consideration the state of Ireland; and by granting her the powerful aid and protection of the Republic, to enable her at once to vindicate her liberty, to humble her tyrant, and to assume that independent station among the nations of the earth for which her soil, her productions and her position, her population and her spirit have designed her."

Finally—after Bantry Bay, the Texel, and Lough Swilly—Tone before his judges thus testified to his faith as a Separatist:

"I mean not to give you the trouble of bringing judicial proof to convict me, legally, of having acted in hostility to the Government of his Britannic Majesty in Ireland. I admit the fact. From my earliest youth I have regarded the connection between Ireland and Great Britain as the curse of the Irish nation, and felt convinced that, whilst it lasted, this country could never be free nor happy. My mind has been confirmed in this opinion by the experience of every succeeding year, and the conclusions which I have drawn from every fact before my eyes. In consequence, I determined to apply all the powers which my individual efforts could move in order to separate the two countries.

"That Ireland was not able, of herself, to throw off the yoke, I knew. I therefore sought for aid wherever it was to be found. In honourable poverty I rejected offers which, to a man in my circumstances, might be considered highly advantageous. I remained faithful to what I thought the cause of my country, and sought in the French Republic an ally to rescue three millions of my countrymen from...."

Here the prisoner was interrupted by the President of the Court-Martial.

III

In order to complete this brief study of Tone's teaching it is necessary to consider him as a democrat. And Tone, the greatest of modern Irish Separatists, is the first and greatest of modern Irish democrats. It was Tone that said:

"Our independence must be had at all hazards. If the men of property will not support us, they must fall: we can support ourselves by the aid of that numerous and respectable class of the community—*the men of no property.*"

In this glorious appeal to Caesar modern Irish democracy has its origin. I have already quoted the secret Manifesto to the Friends of Freedom, attributed to Tone, in which the right to national freedom is made to rest on its true basis, the right to individual freedom. The abstract theory of freedom was not further developed by Tone, who devoted his life to the pursuit of a practical object rather than to the working out of a philosophy. When, however, any question arose which involved the relations of a democracy and an aristocracy, of the people and the gentry ("as they affect to call themselves"), of the "men of no property" and the "men of property," Tone's decision was instant and unerring. The people must rule; if the aristocracy make common cause with the people, so much the better; if not, woe to the aristocracy. One

passage from his Journal, under date April 27th, 1798, says all that need
be said as to the practical question of dealing with a hostile aristocracy
in a national revolution:

"What miserable slaves are the gentry of Ireland!   The only
accusation brought against the United Irishmen by their enemies, is that
they wish to break the connection with England, or, in other words, to
establish the independence of their country—an object in I which surely
the men of property are most interested.   Yet the very sound of
independence seems to have terrified them out of all sense, spirit, or
honesty. If they had one drop of Irish blood in their veins, one grain of
true courage or genuine patriotism in their hearts, they should have been
the first to support this great object; the People would have supported
them; the English government would never have dared to attempt the
measures they have since triumphantly pursued, and continue to pursue;
our Revolution would have been accomplished without a shock, or
perhaps one drop of blood spilled; which now can succeed, if it does
succeed, only by all the calamities of a most furious and sanguinary
contest: for the war in Ireland, whenever it does take place, will not be
an ordinary one. The armies will regard each other not as soldiers, but
as deadly enemies. Who, then, are to blame for this? The United
Irishmen, who set the question afloat, or the English government and
their partisans, the Irish gentry, who resist it? If independence be good
for a country as liberty for an individual, the question will be soon
decided. Why does England so pertinaciously resist our independence?
Is it for love of us—is it because *she* thinks *we* are better as we are? That
single argument, if it stood alone, should determine every honest
Irishman.

"But, it will be said, the United Irishmen extend their views farther;
they go now to a distribution of property, and an agrarian law. I know
not whether they do or no. I am sure in June 1795 when I was forced to
leave the country, they entertained no such ideas. If they have since
taken root among them, the Irish gentry may accuse themselves. Even
then they made themselves parties to the business: not content with
disdaining to hold communications with the United Irishmen, they were

among the foremost of their persecutors: even those who were pleased to denominate themselves patriots were more eager to vilify, and, if they could, to degrade them, than the most devoted and submissive slaves of the English Government. What wonder if the leaders of the United Irishmen, finding themselves not only deserted, but attacked by those who, for every reason, should have been their supporters and fellow-labourers, felt themselves no longer called upon to observe any measures with men only distinguished by the superior virulence of their persecuting spirit? If such men, in the issue, lose their property, they are themselves alone to blame, by deserting the first and most sacred of duties—the duty to their country. They have incurred a wilful forfeiture by disdaining to occupy the station they might have held among the People, and which the People would have been glad to see them fill; they left a vacancy to be seized by those who had more courage, more sense, and more honesty; and not only so, but by this base and interested desertion they furnished their enemies with every argument of justice, policy, and interest, to enforce the system of confiscation.

"The best that can be said in palliation of the conduct of the English party, is that they are content to sacrifice the liberty and independence of their country to the pleasure of revenge, and their own personal security. They see Ireland only in their rent rolls, their places, their patronage, and their pensions. There is not a man among them who, in the bottom of his soul, does not feel that he is a degraded being in comparison of those whom he brands with the names of incendiaries and traitors. It is this stinging reflection which, among other powerful motives, is one of the most active in spurring them on to revenge. Their dearest interests, their warmest passions, are equally engaged. Who can forgive the man that forces him to confess that he is a voluntary slave, and that he has sold for money everything that should be most precious to an honourable heart? that he has trafficked in the liberties of his children and his own, and that he is hired and paid to commit a daily parricide on his country? Yet these are the charges which not a man of that infamous caste can deny to himself before the sacred tribunal of his own conscience. At least the United Irishmen, as I have already said, have a grand, a sublime object in view. Their enemies have not as yet ventured, in the long catalogue of their accusations, to insert the charge of interested motives. Whilst that is the case they may be feared and abhorred, but they can never be despised; and I believe there are few men who do not look upon contempt as the most insufferable of all human evils. Can the English faction say as much? In vain do they crowd together, and think by their numbers to disguise or lessen their infamy. The public sentiment, the secret voice of their own corrupt hearts, has already condemned them. They see their destruction rapidly approaching, and they have the consciousness that when they fall no honest man will pity them. *They shall perish like their own dung; those who have seen them shall say, Where are they?"*

Tone did not propose any general confiscation of private property other than the property of Englishmen in Ireland, and this only after proclamation to the English people, as distinct from the English Government, stating the grounds of the action of the Irish nation and declaring their earnest desire to avoid the effusion of blood; if, after such proclamation, the English people supported the English Government in war upon Ireland, Tone held that the confiscation of English property "would then be an act of strict justice, as the English people would have made themselves parties to the war." Emmet's proposals in 1803 are a fuller and more detailed expression of the mind of revolutionary Ireland on the subject of property. The first decree drafted by Emmet for his Provisional Government was that "tithes are forever abolished, and church lands are the property of the nation;" the second laid down that "from this date all transfers of landed property are prohibited, each person paying his rent until the National Government is established, the national will declared, and the courts of justice be organised;" the third made a like provision with regard to the transfer of bonds and securities; and the fifth decreed the confiscation of the property of Irishmen in the Militia, Yeomanry, or Volunteer corps who, after fourteen days, should be found in arms against the Republic. When we speak of men like Tone and Emmet as "visionaries" and "idealists" we regard only one side of their minds. Both were extraordinarily able men of affairs, masters of all the details of the national, social, and economic positions in their day; and both would have been ruthless in revolution, shedding exactly as much blood as would have been necessary to their purpose. Both, however, were Nationalists first, and revolutionists only in so far as revolution was essential to the establishment of the nation. "We war not against property," said Emmet in his proclamation, "we war against no religious sect, we war not against past opinions or prejudices —we war against English dominion."

One is now in a position to sum up Tone's teaching in a series of propositions:

1. The Irish Nation is One.

2. The Irish Nation, like all Nations, has an indefeasible right to Freedom.

3. Freedom denotes Separation and Sovereignty.

4. The right to National Freedom rests upon the right to Personal Freedom, and true National Freedom guarantees true Personal Freedom.

5. The object of Freedom is the pursuit of the happiness of the Nation and of the individuals that compose the Nation.

6. Freedom is necessary to the happiness and prosperity of the Nation. In the particular case of Ireland, Separation from England is necessary not only to the happiness and prosperity but almost to the continued existence of Ireland, inasmuch as the interests of Ireland and England are fundamentally at variance, and while the two nations are connected England must necessarily predominate.

7. The National Sovereignty implied in National Freedom holds good both externally and internally, *i.e.*, the sovereign rights of the Nation are good as against all other nations and good as

against all parts of the Nation. Hence—

8. The Nation has jurisdiction over lives and property within the Nation.

9. The People are the Nation.

All this Tone taught, not in the dull pages of a treatise, but in the living phrases that dropped from him in his conversation, in his correspondence, in his diaries, in his impassioned pleas for his nation to the Executive Directory of France. Some of the greatest teachers have been literary men only incidentally; but their teaching has none the less the splendour of great literary utterance. The masters of literature do not always label themselves. When a great soul utters a great truth have we not always great literature? That is why the true gospels of the world are always true literature. Those who have preached the divine worth of faith and justice and charity and freedom have done so in glorious and imperishable words: and the reason is that God speaks through them.

That God spoke to Ireland through Tone and through those who, after Tone, have taken up his testimony, that Tone's teaching and theirs is true and great and that no other teaching as to Ireland has any truth or worthiness at all, is a thing upon which I stake all my mortal and all my immortal hopes. And I ask the men and women of my generation to stake their mortal and immortal hopes with me.

THE SPIRITUAL NATION

PREFACE

This Tract continues and develops the argument commenced in "Ghosts," and pursued in "The Separatist Idea," and should be read in connection with those Tracts (which form Nos. 10 and 11 of this series). It is not to be taken as an attempt to represent the whole of Davis's mind or to summarise the whole of his teaching. I consider him here chiefly as one of the Separatist voices.

P. H. PEARSE.

ST. ENDA'S COLLEGE,
RATHFARNHAM,
13th February, 1916.

THE SPIRITUAL NATION

I

I have said that all Irish nationality is implicit in the definition of Tone, and that later teachers have simply made one or other of its truths explicit. It was characteristic of Tone that he stated his case in terms of practical politics. But the statement was none the less a complete statement. To claim independence as the indefeasible right of Ireland is to claim everything for Ireland, all spiritual exaltation and all worldly pomp to which she is entitled. Independence one must understand to include spiritual and intellectual independence as well as political independence; or rather, true political independence requires spiritual and intellectual independence as its basis, or it tends to become unstable, a thing resting merely on interests which change with time and circumstance.

I make a distinction between spiritual and intellectual independence corresponding to the distinction which exists between the spiritual and the intellectual parts in man. The distinction is not easy to express, but it is a real distinction. The soul is not the mind, though it acts by way of the mind, and it is through the mind one gets such glimpses of the soul as are possible. Obviously, a great and beautiful soul may sometimes have to express itself through a very ordinary mind, and a mean or a wicked soul may sometimes express itself through a regal mind; and these possibilities are full of confusion for us, so that when we think we know a man, it is sometimes only his intellect we know, the dialectician or the rhetorician or the idiot in him, and not the strange immortal thing behind. We can learn to know a man's mind, but we can rarely be quite sure that we know his soul. That is a book which only God reads plainly.

Now I think that one may speak of a national soul and of a national mind, and distinguish one from the other, and that this is not merely figurative speaking. When I was a child I believed that there was actually

144

a woman called Erin, and had Mr. Yeats' "Kathleen Ni Houlihan" been then written and had I seen it, I should have taken it not as an allegory, but as a representation of a thing that might happen any day in any house. This I no longer believe as a physical possibility, nor can I convince myself that a friend of mine is right in thinking that there is actually a mystical entity which is the soul of Ireland, and which expresses itself through the mind of Ireland. But I believe that there is really a spiritual tradition which is the soul of Ireland, the thing which makes Ireland a living nation, and that there is such a spiritual tradition corresponding to every true nationality. This spiritual thing is distinct from the intellectual facts in which chiefly it makes its revelation, and it is distinct from them in a way analogous to that in which a man's soul is distinct from his mind. Like other spiritual things, it is independent of the material, whereas the mind is to a large extent dependent upon the material.

I have sometimes thought (but I do not put this forward as a settled belief which I am prepared to defend) that spiritually England and the United States are one nation, while intellectually they are apart.

I am sure that spiritually the Walloons of Belgium are one nation with the French, and that spiritually the Austrians are one nation with the Germans. The spiritual thing which is the essential thing in nationality would seem to reside chiefly in language (if by language we understand literature and folklore as well as sounds and idioms), and to be preserved chiefly by language; but it reveals itself in all the arts, all the institutions, all the inner life, all the actions and goings forth of the nation. It expresses itself fully and magnificently in a great free nation like ancient Greece or modern Germany; it expresses itself only partially and unworthily in an enslaved nation like Ireland. But the soul of the enslaved and broken nation may conceivably be a more splendid thing than the soul of the great free nation; and that is one reason why the enslavements of old and glorious nations that have taken place so often in history are the most terrible things that have ever happened in the world.

If nationality be regarded as the sum of the facts, spiritual and intellectual, which mark off one nation from another, and freedom as the condition which allows those facts full scope and development, it will be seen that both the spiritual and intellectual fact, nationality, and the physical condition, freedom, enter into a proper definition of independence or nationhood. Freedom is a condition which can be lost and won and lost again; nationality is a life which, if once lost, can never be recovered. A nation is a stubborn thing, very hard to kill; but a dead nation does not come back to life, any more than a dead man. There will never again be a Ligurian nation, nor an Aztec nation, nor a Cornish nation.

Irish nationality is an ancient spiritual tradition, and the Irish nation could not die as long as that tradition lived in the heart of one faithful man or woman. But had the last repositor of the Gaelic tradition, the last unconquered Gael, died, the Irish nation was no more. Any free state that might thereafter be erected in Ireland, whatever it might call itself, would certainly not be the historic Irish nation.

Davis was the first of modern Irishmen to make explicit the truth that a nationality is a spirituality. Tone had postulated the great primal truth that Ireland must be free. Davis, accepting that and developing it, stated the truth in its spiritual aspect, that Ireland must be herself; not merely a free self-governing state, but authentically the Irish nation, bearing all the majestic marks of her nationhood. That the nation may live, the Irish life, both the inner life and the outer life, must be conserved. Hence the language, which is the main repository of the Irish life, the folklore, the literature, the music, the art, the social customs, must be conserved. Davis fully realised, with the Gaelic poets, that a nationality connotes a civilisation, and that a civilisation is a body of traditions. He is thus the lineal ancestor of the spiritual movement embodied in our day in the Gaelic League. Tone had set the feet of Ireland on a steep; Davis bade her in her journey remember her old honour and her old sanctity, the fame of Tara and of Clonmacnois. Tone is the Irish nation in action, gay and heroic and terrible; Davis stands by the nation's hearthside, a faithful sentinel.

Ireland is one. Tone had insisted upon the political unity of Ireland. Davis thought of Ireland as a spiritual unity. He recognised that the thing which makes her one is her history, that all her men and women are the heirs of a common past, a past full of spiritual, emotional, and intellectual experiences, which knits them together indissolubly. The nation is thus not a mere agglomeration of individuals, but a living, organic thing, with a body and a soul; twofold in nature, like man, yet one.

Davis's teaching on this head is resumed thus in one of his most lyric paragraphs:

"This country of ours is no sand bank, thrown up by some recent caprice of earth. It is an ancient land, honoured in the archives of civilisation, traceable into antiquity by its piety, its valour, and its sufferings. Every great European race has sent its stream to the river of Irish mind. Long wars, vast organisations, subtle codes, beacon crimes, leading virtues, and self-mighty men were here. If we live influenced by wind and sun and tree, and not by the passions and deeds of the past, we are a thriftless and a hopeless people."

And in another passage he gives the Gaelic League its watchwords:

"Men are ever valued most for peculiar and original qualities. A man who can only talk commonplace, and act according to routine, has little weight. To speak, look, and do what your own soul from its depths orders you are credentials of greatness which all men understand and acknowledge. Such a man's dictum has more influence than the reasoning of an imitative or common-place man. He fills his circle with confidence. He is self-possessed, firm, accurate, and daring. Such men are the pioneers of civilisation and the rulers of the human heart.

"Why should not nations be judged thus? Is not a full indulgence of its natural tendencies essential to a people's greatness?....

"The language which grows up with a people is conformed to their organs, descriptive of their climate, constitution, and manners, mingled inseparably with their history and their soil, fitted beyond any other language to express their prevalent thoughts in the most natural and efficient way.

"To impose another language on such a people is to send their history adrift among the accidents of translation—'tis to tear their identity from all places—'tis to substitute arbitrary signs for picturesque and suggestive names—'tis to cut off the entail of feeling, and separate the people from their forefathers by a deep gulf—'tis to corrupt their very organs, and abridge their power of expression.

"The language of a nation's youth is the only easy and full speech for its manhood and for its age. And when the language of its cradle goes, itself craves a tomb....

"A people without a language of its own is only half a nation. A nation should guard its language more than its territories—'tis a surer barrier, and more important frontier, than fortress or river."

The insistence on the spiritual fact of nationality is Davis's distinctive contribution to political thought in Ireland, but it is not the whole of Davis. It has become common to regard him as the type of the "intellectual Nationalist," who is distinguished from that other and more troublesome person, the political irreconcilable. And there is a passage of Gavan Duffy's which lends countenance to this. But the view is a false one as regards Davis and a false one as regards the irreconcilables. Davis accepts the political doctrine of the irreconcilables, and the irreconcilables accept the spiritual teaching of Davis. The two teachings are facets of one truth. And Davis saw the whole truth. He saw that Ireland must be independent of England. It is necessary for me to prove this.

II

First to brush away a cobweb. It has been maintained that Davis would have been satisfied with what is called a Federal settlement. The only authority for this view seems to be the following passage in Gavan Duffy's *Young Ireland*: "Some of them [the "moderate men" who are always with us] came to the conclusion that an Irish Legislature for purely Irish purposes, as a sort of chapel of ease to the Imperial Parliament, ought to be demanded. Mr. Sharman Crawford, on behalf of himself and others unnamed, but understood to include members of both Houses, announced that he desired the establishment of a Federal Union between England and Ireland. He wished to see a 'local body for the purpose of local legislation, combined with an Imperial representation for Imperial purposes;' and he considered that no 'Act of the Imperial Parliament having a separate action as regards Ireland should be a law in Ireland unless passed or confirmed by her own legislative body.' It is a fact worthy to be pondered on that Davis was favourable to this experiment. He desired and would have fought for independence, but he was so little of what in later times has been called 'an irreconcilable,' that such an alternative was not the first, but the last, resource he contemplated. He desired to unite and elevate the whole nation, and he would have accepted Federation as the scheme most likely to accustom and reconcile Protestants to self-government, and as a sure step towards legislative independence in the end."

Thus Duffy on Davis. In a moment we shall let Davis speak for himself.

When Davis, in 1842, leaped into his place in Irish politics as the chief influence on the staff of the *Nation*, all Ireland was organised in the greatest constitutional movement and under the greatest constitutional leader known to history. The demand of that movement was for Repeal of the Union. Separatism was only an inarticulate faith of the common people, remembered for the rest by a few noble old men like Robert Holmes, by a few fiery exiles like Miles Byrne. The *Nation* ranged itself under O'Connell's banner, though from the beginning its writers descried a wider horizon than O'Connell ever did or could. In 1843 O'Connell made what Duffy calls the "portentous" announcement that he felt "a preference for the Federative plan, as tending more to the utility of Ireland and the maintenance of the connection with England than the proposal of simple Repeal." Davis was away from Dublin, but Duffy, in a personal letter to O'Connell, which he printed as a leading article in the *Nation*, objected to the change of policy foreshadowed, and insisted that "the Repeal Association had no more right to alter the constitution on which its members were recruited than the Irish Parliament had to surrender its functions without consulting its constituents." When Davis returned to town he "cordially accepted," says Duffy, the policy of resistance.

Davis soon spoke in the *Nation*. He welcomed the overtures of the Federalists, but as to his own position and the *Nation's* position he had no doubt. He settled it in one sentence:

"Let the Federalists be an independent and respected party, the repealers an unbroken league—our stand is with the latter."

So that, as between Federalism and Repeal, Davis defined himself a Repealer. But was he not something more?

Davis died before Young Ireland had reached its full political stature or found its full political voice. Just as the United Irishmen spoke first the language of constitutionalism, so did the Young Irelanders. Davis, as their spokesman, spoke their official language, but he hinted, and more than hinted, at a fuller utterance. Mitchel, who took up Davis's post in 1845, spoke the fuller utterance, but at his fullest he said nothing that had not been just as fully implied by Davis. For Davis was a Separatist.

Davis wrote of Tone that he was "the wisest...of our last generation." And he applied the adjective "wise" to Tone in contradistinction to Grattan, whom in the same sentence he called "the most sublime" of the last generation. Now, Tone was the Separatist and Grattan was the British-Connectionist. When Davis wrote of Tone that he was wiser than Grattan he did not mean that he was more worldly-wise, that he was an abler business man; for Tone died a pauper and Grattan died wealthy; Tone died in a dungeon and his body with difficulty obtained Christian burial, Grattan was buried with pomp in Westminster Abbey. Davis meant that Tone was a wiser statesman than Grattan, that Separation was a wiser policy for Ireland than British-Connectionism. And he meant that he, Davis, was a disciple of Tone.

In the light of this recognition such a passage as the following, which were otherwise mere froth and foam, becomes full of substance:

"This is the history of two years never surpassed in importance and honour. This is a history which our sons shall pant over and envy. This is a history which pledges as to perseverance. This is a history which guarantees success.

"Energy, patience, generosity, skill, tolerance, enthusiasm, created and decked the agitation. The world attended us with its thoughts and prayers. The graceful genius of Italy and the profound intellect of Germany paused to wish us well. The fiery heart of France tolerated our unarmed effort, and preferred its aid. America sent us money, thought, love—she made herself a part of Ireland in her passions and her organisations. From London to the wildest settlement which throbs in the tropics or shivers nigh the Pole, the empire of our mis-ruler was shaken by our effort. To all earth we proclaimed our wrongs. To man and God we made oath that we would never cease to strive till an Irish nation stood supreme on this island. The genius which had organised us, the energy which laboured, the wisdom that taught, the manhood which rose up, the patience which obeyed, the faith which swore, and the valour that strained for action, are here still, experienced, recruited, resolute.

"The future shall realise the promise of the past."

This is Davis's passionate appeal to his own; and here is how he talks to the enemy:

"And if England will do none of these things, will she allow us, for good or ill, to govern ourselves, and see if we cannot redress our own griefs? 'No, never, never.' she says, 'though all Ireland cried for it—never! Her fields shall be manured with the shattered limbs of her sons, and her hearths quenched in their blood; but never, while England has a ship or a soldier, shall Ireland be free.'

"And this is your answer? We shall see—we shall see!

"And now, Englishmen, listen to us! Though you were to-morrow to give us the best tenures on earth—though you were to equalise Presbyterian, Catholic, and Episcopalian —though you were to give us the amplest representation in your Senate—though you were to restore our absentees, disencumber us of your debt, and redress every one of our fiscal wrongs—and though, in addition to all this, you plundered the treasuries of the world to lay gold at our feet, and exhausted the resources of your genius to do us worship and honour—still we tell you—we tell you, in the names liberty and country—we tell you, in the name of enthusiastic hearts, thoughtful souls, and fearless spirits—we tell you, by the past, the present, and the future, we would spurn your gifts, if the condition were that Ireland should remain a province. We tell you, and all whom it may concern, come what may—bribery or deceit, justice, policy, or war—we tell you, in the name of Ireland, that Ireland shall be a nation!"

Now, when Davis told England that, come bribery or deceit, justice, policy, or war, *Ireland shall be a nation*; when Davis reminded the men of Ireland that they had sworn "never to cease to strive until '*an Irish nation stood supreme on this island*,'" he meant what he said. By an Irish nation "standing supreme" he did really mean a Sovereign Irish State living her own life, mistress of her own destinies, defending her own shores, with her ambassadors in foreign capitals and her flag on the seas. He tells us that he meant this. The most important of Davis's political articles are those in which he develops a foreign policy for Ireland. And the most significant passage in all Davis's political writings is this (the italics are his own):

"Again, it is peculiarly needful for *Ireland* to have a Foreign Policy. Intimacy with the great powers will guard us from English interference. Many of the minor German States were too deficient in numbers, boundaries, and wealth to have outstood the despotic ages of Europe, but for those foreign alliances, which, whether resting on friendship or a desire to preserve the balance of power, secured them against their rapacious neighbours. And now time has given its sanction to their continuance, and the progress of localisation guarantees their future safety. When Ireland is a nation she will not, with her vast population and her military character, require such alliances as a *security* against English *re-conquest*; but they will be useful in banishing any *dreams of invasion* which might *otherwise* haunt the brain of our old enemy."

As a Separatist utterance this is as plenary as anything in Tone. The "Irish nation" contemplated by Davis presupposed the breaking of the

English connection, for it was to have military resources sufficient to guard against "an English *re-conquest*" and was to seek foreign alliances in order to banish any "*dreams of invasion*" cherished by "our old enemy."

To Davis, as to Tone, England was "the enemy." Davis was as anti-English as Tone, and, for all his gentleness and charity, more bitter in the expression of his anti-Englishism than Tone was. To him the English language was "a mongrel of a thousand breeds." Modern English literature was "surpassed" by French literature.

"France is an apostle of liberty—England the turnkey of the world. France is the old friend, England the old foe, of Ireland. From one we may judge all. England has defamed *all other countries* in order to make us and her other slaves content in our fetters."

Davis saw as clearly as Tone saw that the English connection is the never-failing source of Ireland's political evils, and he stated his perception as clearly as Tone did.

"He who fancies some intrinsic objection to our nationality to lie in the co-existence of two languages, three or four great sects, and a dozen different races in Ireland, will learn that in Hungary, Switzerland, Belgium, and America, different languages, creeds, and races flourish kindly side by side, and he will seek in English intrigues the real well of the bitter woes of Ireland."

Again:

"Germany, France, and America teach us that English economics are not fit for a nation beginning to establish a trade, though they may be for an old and plethoric trader; and, therefore, that English and Irish trading interests are directly opposed."

Yet again:

"The land tenures of France, Norway and Prussia are the reverse of England's. They resemble our own old tenures; they better suit our character and our wants than the loose holdings and servile wages system of modern England."

And finally:

"We must believe and act up to the lesson taught by reason and history, that England is our interested and implacable enemy—a tyrant to her dependants—a calumniator of her neighbours, and both the despot and the defamer of Ireland for near seven centuries."

It has thus been established, and established by his own words, first, that as between Federalism and Repeal Davis was a Repealer: but, secondly, that as between Repeal and Separation Davis was a Separatist. In other words, he held the national position which Tone held, which Lalor and Mitchel held, which the Fenians held, which the Irish Volunteers hold. The fact that he would have accepted and worked on with Repeal in no wise derogates from his status as a Separatist, any more than the fact that many of us would have accepted Home Rule (or even Devolution) and worked on with it derogates from our status as Separatists. Home Rule to us would have been a means to an end: Repeal to Davis would have been a means to an end.

In one of the phrases in which such men as he give watchwords to the generations, a phrase which strangely anticipates the most famous of Parnell's phrases, Davis tells us what that end was:

"Ireland's aspiration is for unbounded nationality."

I have shown what he meant by "unbounded nationality;" he meant sovereign nationhood, he meant spiritual, intellectual, and political independence. The word "nationality" I have used here and elsewhere for the inner thing which is a nation's soul, and the word "nationhood" I have made to include both that inner thing and the outer status, political independence. It is obvious that Davis uses the term "nationality" in the sense in which I use the term "nationhood," for if he meant only the inner spiritual thing his phrase would be meaningless.

In order to the proper adjustment of values we may now usefully set down:

First, that the Federalism with which O'Connell dallied for a moment, but which Davis and Young Ireland protested against and O'Connell promptly disowned, abandoning it, indeed, with the contemptuous phrase: "federalism is not worth *that* (snapping his fingers), contemplated a domestic Irish legislature to deal with domestic Irish affairs, adequate Irish representation in an Imperial Parliament, and *power of veto in the Irish Parliament over acts of the Imperial Parliament having a separate action as regards Ireland.* It was thus a vastly bigger thing than modern Home Rule, which reserves everything of real importance from the jurisdiction of the Irish Parliament, which, far from giving the Irish Parliament a veto over the acts of the Imperial Parliament regarding Ireland, gives the Imperial Parliament a veto over all acts of the Irish Parliament, and which preserves intact the power of the Imperial Parliament to pass all sorts of laws binding Ireland and to impose all sorts of taxation on Ireland, the Irish representation in the Imperial Parliament to be a negligible quantity.

Secondly, that the Repeal of the Union, which, apart from his momentary aberration into Federalism, was O'Connell's life-long demand, contemplated a Sovereign Irish Parliament co-ordinate with the English Parliament and with absolute control of Irish taxation; and while there was to be a common king, army, navy, and foreign policy, not a penny was to be raised from Ireland for the financing of those concerns except by the vote of the Irish Parliament. It will be seen that Repeal was as much a bigger thing than the Home Rule of 1914 as O'Connell was a greater man than Mr. Redmond. Repeal contemplated a sovereign co-ordinate Parliament; Home Rule specifically contemplated a subordinate Parliament. Under Repeal the Imperial Parliament would have had no jurisdiction over any man of Ireland, over any sod of Ireland's soil, over any shilling of Ireland's money; under Home Rule the jurisdiction of the Imperial Parliament over these things and all other things in Ireland was to have been absolute, for the Act laid down (Clause

One) that "the supreme power and authority of the Parliament of the United Kingdom shall remain unaffected and undiminished over all persons, matters and things in Ireland, and every part thereof."

Thirdly, that even the noble and semi-independent status which would have been secured to Ireland by Repeal was not sufficient for Tone, who rose against the very constitution which Repeal sought to restore; for Davis, who aspired to "unbounded nationality;" for Lalor, whose object was "not to repeal the Union but the conquest," and who "for Repeal had never gone into agitation and would never go into insurrection;" for Mitchel, who, far from accepting that partnership in the British Empire on which Repeal was founded, avowed it as his aim in life to utterly destroy the British Empire. What was it that these men wanted? They wanted Separation; they wanted "to BREAK the connection with England, the never-failing source of all our political evils." Davis's principles, then, were Tone's; and as to methods. That Davis would have achieved Irish nationhood by peaceful means if he could, is undoubted. Let it not be a reproach against Davis. Obviously, if a nation can obtain its freedom without bloodshed, it is its duty so to obtain it. Those of us who believe that, in the circumstances of Ireland, it is not possible to obtain our freedom without bloodshed will admit thus much. If England, after due pressure, were to say to us, "Here, take Ireland," no one would be so foolish as to answer, "No, we'd rather fight you for it." But things like that do not happen. One must fight, or at least be ready to fight. And Davis knew this:

"The tribune's tongue and poet's pen
  May sow the seed in slavish men;
  But 'tis the soldier's sword alone
  Can reap the harvest when 'tis grown."

And Davis was ready to fight. No one knew better than he that England would yield only to force or the threat of force; and that England, having once yielded, could be held to her bargain only by force. The nation that he visioned was to be an armed nation; and armed for the precise purpose of preventing any "reconquest" by England. No one saw more clearly than Davis that Ireland made her mistake of mistakes when her Volunteers abdicated their arms. Referring to Madden's defence of Grattan against Flood on the question of Simple Repeal, Davis writes:

"This is unanswerable, but Grattan should have gone further. The revolution was effected mainly by the Volunteers, whom he had inspired; arms could alone have preserved the constitution. Flood was wrong in setting value on one form—Grattan in relying on any; but before and after '82 Flood seems to have had glimpses that the question was one of might, as well as of right, and that national laws could not last under such an alien army.

"Taken as military representatives, the Convention at the Rotunda was even more valuable than as a civic display. Mr. Madden censures Grattan for having been an elaborate neutral during these Reform dissensions; but that the result of *such* neutrality ruined the Convention proves the comparative want of power in Flood, who could have governed Convention in spite of the rascally English and the feeble Irish Whigs. Oh, had Tone been in that council!"

The astonishing thing about Davis is that, writing in the still constitutional *Nation* of 1842-5, he was able to express his Separatist faith so clearly, and to avow so openly his readiness to fight for that faith. It took Duffy three years longer to reach the point which had been reached in 1845 by his dead friend.

III

If we accept the definition of Irish freedom as "the Rights of Man in Ireland" we shall find it difficult to imagine an apostle of Irish freedom who is not a democrat. One loves the freedom of men because one loves men. There is therefore a deep humanism in every true Nationalist. There was a deep humanism in Tone; and there was a deep humanism in Davis. The sorrow of the people affected Davis like a personal sorrow. He had more respect for aristocracy than Tone had (Tone had none), and would have been less ruthless in a revolution than Tone would have been. But he was a democrat in this truest sense, that he loved the people, and his love of the people was an essential part of the man and of his Nationalism. Even his rhetoric (for Davis, unlike Tone, was a little rhetorical) cannot disguise the sincerity of such passages as this:

"Think of the long, long patience of the people—their toils supporting you—their virtues shaming you—their huts, their hunger, their disease.

"To whosoever God hath given a heart less cold than stone, these truths must cry day and night. Oh! how they cross us like Banshees when we would range free on the mountain—how, as we walk in the evening light amid flowers, they startle us from rest of mind! Ye nobles! whose houses are as gorgeous as the mote's (which dwelleth in the sunbeam) —ye strong and haughty squires—ye dames exuberant with tingling blood—ye maidens whom no splendour has yet spoiled, will ye not think of the poor?..."

The real Davis must have been a greater man even than the Davis of the essays, or the Davis of the songs. In literary expression Davis was immature; in mind he was ripe beyond all his contemporaries. I cannot call him a very great prose writer; I am not sure that I can call him a poet at all. But I can call him a very great man, one of our greatest men. None of his contemporaries had any doubt about his greatness. He was the greatest influence among them, and the noblest influence; and he has been the greatest and noblest influence in Irish history since Tone. He was not Young Ireland's most powerful prose writer: Mitchel was that. He was not Young Ireland's truest poet: Mangan was that, or, if not Mangan, Ferguson. He was not Young Ireland's ablest man of affairs: Duffy was that. He was not Young Ireland's most brilliant orator: Meagher was that. Nevertheless, "Davis was our true leader," said Duffy; and when Davis died—the phrase is again Duffy's—"it seemed as if the sun had gone out of the heavens." "The loss of this rare and noble Irishman," said Mitchel, "has never been repaired, neither to his country nor to his friends." What was it that made Davis so great in the eyes of two such men, and two such different men, as Duffy and Mitchel? It must have been the man's immortal soul. The highest form of genius is the genius for sanctity, the genius for noble life and thought. That genius was Davis's. Character is the greatest thing in a man; and Davis's character was such as the Apollo Belvidere is said to be in the physical order—in his presence all men stood more erect. The Romans had a noble word which summed up all moral beauty and all private and civic valour: the word *virtus*. If English had as noble a word as that it would be the word to apply to the thing which made Thomas Davis so great a man.

THE SOVEREIGN PEOPLE

PREFACE

This pamphlet concludes the examination of the Irish definition of freedom which I promised in "Ghosts." For my part, I have no more to say.

P. H. PEARSE.

ST. ENDA'S COLLEGE,
RATHFARNHAM,
31st March, 1916.

THE SOVEREIGN PEOPLE

I

National independence involves national sovereignty. National sovereignty is twofold in its nature. It is both internal and external. It implies the sovereignty of the nation over all its parts, over all men and things within the nation; and it implies the sovereignty of the nation as against all other nations. Nationality is a spiritual fact; but nationhood includes physical freedom, and physical power in order to the maintenance of physical freedom, as well as the spiritual fact of nationality. This physical freedom is necessary to the healthy life, and may even be necessary to the continued existence of the nation. Without it the nation droops, withers, ultimately perhaps dies; only a very steadfast nation, a nation of great spiritual and intellectual strength like Ireland, can live for more than a few generations in its absence, and without it even so stubborn a nation as Ireland would doubtless ultimately perish. Physical freedom, in brief, is necessary to sane and vigorous life; for physical freedom means precisely control of the conditions that are necessary to sane and vigorous life. It is obvious that these things are partly material, and that therefore national freedom involves control of the material things which are essential to the continued physical life and freedom of the nation. So that the nation's sovereignty extends not only to all the material possessions of the nation, the nation's soil and all its resources, all wealth and all wealth-producing processes within the nation. In other words, no private right to property is good as against the public right of the nation. But the nation is under a moral obligation so to exercise its public right as to secure strictly equal rights and liberties to every man and woman within the nation. The whole is entitled to pursue the happiness and prosperity of the whole, but this is to be pursued exactly for the end that each of the individuals composing the whole may enjoy happiness and prosperity, the maximum amount of happiness and prosperity consistent with the happiness and prosperity of all the rest.

One may reduce all this to a few simple propositions:

1. The end of freedom is human happiness.

2. The end of national freedom is individual freedom; therefore, individual happiness.

3. National freedom implies national sovereignty.

4. National sovereignty implies control of all the moral and material resources of the nation.

I have insisted upon the spiritual fact of nationality; I have insisted upon the necessity of physical freedom in order to the continued preservation of that spiritual fact in a living people; I now insist upon the necessity of complete Control of the material resources of the nation in order to the completeness of that physical freedom. And here I think I give what has been called "the material basis of freedom" its proper place and importance. A nation's material resources are not the nation, any more than a man's food is the man; but the material resources as necessary to the nation's life as the man's food to the man's life.

And I claim that the nation's sovereignty over the nation's material resources is absolute; but that obviously such sovereignty must be exercised for the good of the nation and without prejudice to the rights of other nations, since national sovereignty, like everything else on earth, is subject to the laws of morality.

Now, the good of the nation means ultimately the good of the individual men and women who compose the nation. Physically considered, what does a nation consist of? It consists of its men and women; of all its men and women, without any exceptions. Every man and every woman within the nation has normally equal rights, but a man or a woman may forfeit his or her rights by turning recreant to the nation. No class in the nation has rights superior to those of any other class. No class in the nation is entitled to privileges beyond any other class except with the consent of the nation. The right and privilege to make laws or to administer laws does not reside in any class within the nation; it resides in the whole nation, that is, in the whole people, and can be lawfully exercised only by those to whom it is delegated by the whole people. The right to the control of the material resources of a nation does not reside in any individual or in any class of individuals; it resides in the whole people and can be lawfully exercised only by those to whom it is delegated by the whole people, and in the manner in which the whole people ordains. Once more, no individual right is good as against the right of the whole people; but the people, in exercising its sovereign rights, is morally bound to consider individual rights, to do equity between itself and each of the individuals that compose it as well as to see that equity is done between individual and individual.

To insist upon the sovereign control of the nation over all the property within the nation is not to disallow the right to private property. It is for the nation to determine to what extent private property may be held by its members, and in what items of the nation's material resources private property shall be allowed. A nation may, for instance, determine, as the free Irish nation determined and enforced for many centuries, that private ownership shall not exist in land; that the whole of a nation's soil is the public property of the nation. A nation may determine, as many modern nations have determined, that all the means of transport within a nation, all its railways and waterways, are the public property of the nation to be administered by the nation for the general benefit. A nation may go further and determine that all sources of wealth whatsoever are the property of the nation, that each individual shall give his service for the nation's good, and shall be adequately provided for by the nation, and that all surplus wealth shall go to the national treasury to be expended on national purposes, rather than be accumulated by private persons. There is nothing divine or sacrosanct in any of these arrangements; they are matters of purely human concern, matters for discussion and adjustment between the members of a nation, matters to be decided upon finally by the nation as a whole; and matters in which the nation as a whole can revise or reverse its decision whenever it seems good in the common interests to do so. I do not disallow the right to private property; but I insist that all property is held subject to the national sanction.

And I come back again to this: that the people are the nation; the whole people, all its men and women; and that laws made or acts done by anybody purporting to represent the people but not really authorised by the people, either expressly or impliedly, to represent them and to act for them do not bind the people; are a usurpation, an impertinence, a nullity. For instance, a Government of capitalists, or a Government of clerics, or a Government of lawyers, or a Government of tinkers, or a Government of red-headed men, or a Government of men born on a Tuesday, does not represent the people, and cannot bind the people, unless it is expressly or impliedly chosen and accepted by the people to represent and act for them; and in that case it becomes the lawful government of the people, and continues such until the people withdraw their mandate. Now, the people, if wise, will not choose the makers and administrators of their laws on such arbitrary and fantastic grounds as the possession of capital, or the possession of red heads, or the having been born on a Tuesday; a Government chosen in such a manner, or preponderatingly representing (even if not so deliberately chosen) capitalists, red-headed men, or men born on a Tuesday will inevitably legislate and govern in the interests of capitalists, red-headed men, or men born on a Tuesday, as the case may be. The people, if wise, will choose as the makers and administrators of their laws men and women actually and fully representative of all the men and women of the nation, the men and women of no property equally with the men and women of property; they will regard such an accident as the possession of "property," "capital," "wealth" in any shape, the possession of what is called "a stake in the country," as conferring no more right to represent the people than would the accident of possessing a red head or the accident of having been born on a Tuesday. And in order that the people may be able to choose as a legislation and as a government men and women really and fully representative of themselves, they will keep the choice actually or virtually in the hands of the whole people; in other words, while, in the exercise of their sovereign rights they may, if they will, delegate the actual choice to some body among them, *i.e.*, adopt a "restricted franchise," they will, if wise, adopt the widest possible franchise—give a vote to every adult man and woman of sound mind. To restrict the franchise in any respect is to prepare the way for some future usurpation of the rights of the sovereign people. The people, that is, the whole people, must remain sovereign not only in theory, but in fact.

I assert, then, the divine right of the people, "God's grant to Adam and his poor children forever," to have and to hold this good green earth. And I assert the sovereignty and the sanctity of the nations, which are the people embodied and organised. The nation is a natural division, as natural as the family, and as inevitable. That is one reason why a nation is holy and why an empire is not holy. A nation is knit together by natural ties, ties mystic and spiritual, and ties human and kindly; an empire is at best held together by ties of mutual interest, and at worst by brute force. The nation is the family in large; an empire is a commercial corporation in large. The nation is of God; the empire is of man—if it be not of the devil.

II

The democratic truths that I have just stated are implicit in Tone and in Davis, though there was this difference between the two men, that Tone had a manly contempt for "the gentry (as they affect to call themselves)," while Davis had a little sentimental regard for them. But Davis loved the people, as every Nationalist must love the people, seeing that the people are the nation; his nationalism was not mere devotion to an abstract idea, it was a devotion to the actual men and women who make up this nation of Ireland, a belief in their rights, and a resolve to establish them as the owners of Ireland and the masters of all her destinies. There is no other sort of nationalism than this, the nationalism which believes in and seeks to enthrone the sovereign people. Tone had appealed to "that numerous and respectable class, the men of no property," and in that gallant and characteristic phrase he had revealed his perception of a great historic truth, namely, that in Ireland "the gentry (as they affect to call themselves)" have uniformly been corrupted by England, and the merchants and middle-class capitalists have, when not corrupted, been uniformly intimidated, whereas the common people have for the most part remained unbought and unterrified. It is, in fact, true that the repositories of the Irish tradition, as well the spiritual tradition of nationality as the kindred tradition of stubborn physical resistance to England, have been the great, splendid, faithful, common people—that dumb multitudinous throng which sorrowed during the penal night, which bled in '98, which starved in the Famine; and which is here still—what is left of it—unbought and unterrified. Let no man be mistaken as to who will be lord in Ireland when Ireland is free. The people will be lord and master. The people who wept in Gethsemane, who trod the sorrowful way, who died naked on a cross, who went down into hell, will rise again glorious and immortal, will sit on the right hand of God, and will come in the end to give judgment, a judge just and terrible.

Tone sounded the gallant *reveillé* of democracy in Ireland. The man who gave it its battle-cries was James Fintan Lalor. Lalor was a fiery spirit, as of some angelic missionary, imprisoned for a few years in a very frail tenement, drawing his earthly breath in pain; but strong with a great spiritual strength and gifted with a mind which had the trenchant beauty of steel. What he had to say for his people (and for all mankind) was said in a very few words. This gospel of the Sovereign People that Fintan Lalor delivered is the shortest of the gospels; but so precious is it, so pregnant with meaning in its every word, that to express its sense one would have to quote it almost as it stands; which indeed one could do in a tract a very little longer than this. No one who wrote as little as Lalor has ever written so well. In his first letter he laments that he has never learned the art of literary expression; in "The Faith of a Felon" he says that he has all his life been destitute of books. Commonly, it is by reading and writing that a man learns to write greatly. Lalor, who had read little and written nothing, wrote greatly from the moment he began to write. The Lord God must have inspired the poor crippled recluse, for no mortal man could of himself have uttered the things he uttered.

James Fintan Lalor, in Duffy's phrase, "announced himself" in Irish politics in 1847, and he announced himself "with a voice of assured confidence and authority." In a letter to Duffy, which startled all the Young Irelanders and which set Mitchel's heart on fire, he declared himself one of the people, one who therefore knew the people: and he told the young men that there was neither strength nor even a disposition among the people to carry on O'Connell's Repeal, but that there was strength in the people to carry national independence if national independence were associated with something else.

"A mightier question is in the land—one beside which Repeal dwarfs down to a petty parish question; one on which Ireland may not alone try her own right but try the right of the world; on which she would be not merely an asserter of old principles, often asserted, and better asserted before her, an humble and feeble imitator and follower of other countries—but an original inventor, propounder, and propagandist, in the van of the earth, and heading the nations; on which her success or her failure alike would never be forgotten by man, but would make her for ever a lodestar of history; on which Ulster would be not 'on her flank' but at her side, and on which, better and best of all, she need not plead in humble petitions her beggarly wrongs and how beggarly she bore them, nor plead any right save the right of her MIGHT....

"Repeal may perish with all who support it sooner than I will consent to be fettered on this question, or to connect myself with any organised body that would ban or merge, in favour of Repeal or any other measure, that greatest of all our rights on this side of heaven—God's grant to Adam and his poor children for ever, when He sent them from Eden in His wrath and bid them go work for their bread. Why should I name it?"

His proposals as to means thrilled the young orators and debaters as the ringing voice of an angel might thrill them:

"As regards the use of none but legal means, any means and all means might be made illegal by Act of Parliament, and such pledge, therefore, is passive obedience. As to the pledge of abstaining from the use of any but moral force, I am quite willing to take such pledge, if, and provided, the English Government agree to take it also; but 'if not, not.' Let England pledge not to argue the question by the prison, the convict-ship, or the halter; and I will readily pledge not to argue it in any form of physical logic. But dogs tied and stones loose are no bargain. Let the stones be given up; or unmuzzle the wolf-dog...."

At Duffy's invitation Lalor developed his doctrines in two letters to the *Nation*, one addressed to the landlords and one to the people. To the landlords he spoke this ominous warning:

"Refuse it [to be Irishmen], and you commit yourself to the position of paupers, to the mercy of English Ministers and English members; you throw your very existence on English support, which England soon may find too costly to afford; you lie at the feet of events; you lie in the way of a people and the movement of events and the march of a people shall be over you."

The essence of Lalor's teaching is that the right to the material ownership of a nation's soil co-exists with the right to make laws for the nation and that both are inherent in the same authority, the Sovereign People. He held in substance that Separation from England would be valueless unless it put the people—the actual people and not merely certain rich men—of Ireland in effectual ownership and possession of the soil of Ireland; as for a return to the *status quo* before 1800, it was to him impossible and unthinkable. When Mitchel's *United Irishman* was suppressed in 1848, Martin's *Irish Felon*, with Lalor as its standard-bearer and spokesman, stepped into the breach; and in an article entitled "The Rights of Ireland" in the first issue of that paper (June 24, 1848) Lalor delivered the new gospel. A long passage must be quoted in full; but it can be quoted without any comment, for it is self-luminous:

"Without agreement as to our objects we cannot agree on the course we should follow. It is requisite the paper should have but one purpose; and the public should understand what that purpose is. Mine is not to repeal the Union, or restore Eighty- two. This is not the year '82, this is the year '48. For repeal I never went into 'Agitation,' and will not go into insurrection. On that question, I refuse to arm, or to act in any mode; and the country refuses. O'Connell made no mistake when he pronounced it not worth the price of one drop of blood; and for myself, I regret it was not left in the hands of Conciliation Hall, whose lawful property it was, and is. Moral force and repeal, the means and the purpose, were just fitted to each other—*Arcades ambo*, balmy Arcadians both. When the means were limited, it was only proper and necessary to limit the purpose. When the means were enlarged, that purpose ought to have been enlarged also. Repeal, in its vulgar meaning, I look on as utterly impracticable by any mode of action whatever; and the constitution of '82 was absurd, worthless, and worse than worthless. The English Government will never concede or surrender to any species of moral force whatsoever; and the country-peasantry will never arm and fight for it—neither will I. If I am to stake life and fame, it must assuredly be for something better and greater, more likely to last, more likely to succeed, and better worth success. And a stronger passion, a higher purpose, a nobler and more needful enterprise is fermenting in the hearts of the people. A mightier question moves Ireland to-day than that of merely repealing the Act of Union. Not the constitution that Wolfe Tone died to abolish, but the constitution that Tone died to obtain— independence; full and absolute independence for this island, and for every man within this island. Into no movement that would leave an enemy's garrison in possession of all our lands, masters of our liberties, our lives, and all our means of life and happiness—into no such movement will a single man of the greycoats enter with an armed hand, whatever the town population may do. On a wider fighting field, with stronger positions and greater resources than are afforded by the paltry question of Repeal, must we close for our final struggle with England, or sink and surrender.

"Ireland her own—Ireland her own, and all therein, from the sod to the sky. The soil of Ireland for the people of Ireland, to have and hold from God alone who gave it—to have and to hold to them and their heirs for ever, without suit or service, faith or fealty, rent or render, to any power under Heaven.... When a greater and more ennobling enterprise is on foot, every inferior and feebler project or proceeding will soon be left in the hands of old women, of dastards, imposters, swindlers, and imbeciles. All the strength and manhood of the island—all the courage, energies, and ambition—all the passion, heroism, and chivalry—all the strong men and strong minds—all those that make revolutions will quickly desert it, and throw themselves into the greater movement, throng into the larger and loftier undertaking, and flock round the banner that flies nearest the sky. There go the young, the gallant, the gifted, the daring; and there, too, go the wise. For wisdom knows that in national action *littleness* is more fatal than the wildest rashness; that greatness of object is essential to greatness of effort, strength, and success; that a revolution ought never to take its stand on low or narrow ground, but seize on the broadest and highest ground it can lay hands on; and that a petty enterprise seldom succeeds. Had America aimed or declared for less than independence, she would, probably, have failed, and been a fettered slave to-day.

"Not to repeal the Union, then, but the conquest—not to disturb or dismantle the empire, but to abolish it utterly for ever—not to fall back on '82, but act up to '48—not to resume or restore an old constitution, but found a new nation and raise up a free people, and strong as well as free, and secure as well as strong, based on a peasantry rooted like rocks in the soil of the land—this is my object, as I hope it is yours; and this, you may rest assured, is the easier, as it is the nobler and more pressing enterprise."

Lalor proceeds to develop his teaching as to the ownership of the soil of Ireland by its people:

"The principle I state, and mean to stand upon, is this: that the entire ownership of Ireland, moral and material, up to the sun and down to the centre, is vested of right in the people of Ireland; that they, and none but they, are the land-owners and law-makers of this island; that all laws are null and void not made by them, and all titles to land invalid not conferred or confirmed by them; and that this full right of ownership may

171

and ought to be asserted by any and all means which God has put in the power of man. In other, if not plainer words, I hold and maintain that the entire soil of a country belongs of right to the entire people of that country, and is the rightful property, not of any one class, but of the nation at large, in full effective possession, to let to whom they will, on whatever tenures, terms, rents, services, and conditions they will; one condition, however, being unavoidable and essential, the condition that the tenant shall bear full, true, and undivided fealty and allegiance to the nation, and the laws of the nation whose lands he holds, and own no allegiance whatsoever to any other prince, power, or people, or any obligation of obedience or respect to their will, orders, or laws. I hold, further, and firmly believe, that the enjoyment by the people of this right of first ownership of the soil is essential to the vigour and vitality of all other rights, to their validity, efficacy, and value; to their secure possession and safe exercise. For let no people deceive themselves, or be deceived by the words, and colours, and phrases, and forms of a mock freedom, by constitutions, and charters, and articles, and franchise. These things are paper and parchment, waste and worthless. Let laws and institutions say what they will, this fact will be stronger than all laws, and prevail against them—the fact that those who own your lands will make your laws, and command your liberties and your lives. But this is tyranny and slavery; tyranny in its widest scope and worst shape; slavery of body and soul, from the cradle to the coffin—slavery with all its horrors, and with none of its physical comforts and security; even as it is in Ireland, where the whole community is made up of tyrants, slaves, and slave-drivers...."

As to the question of dealing with landowners, Lalor re-echoes Tone and Davis:

"There are, however, many landlords, perhaps, and certainly a few, not fairly chargeable with the crimes of their order; and you may think it hard they should lose their lands. But recollect the principle I assert would make Ireland, *in fact*, as she is *of right*, mistress and queen of all those lands; that she, poor lady, had ever a soft heart and grateful

172

disposition; and that she may, if she please, in reward of allegiance, confer new titles or confirm the old. Let us crown her a queen; and then—let her do with her lands as a queen may do.

"In the case of any existing interest, of what nature soever, I feel assured that no question but one would need to be answered. Does the owner of that interest assent to swear allegiance to the people of Ireland, and to hold in fee from the Irish nation? If he assent he may be assured he will suffer no loss. No eventual or permanent loss I mean; for some temporary loss he must assuredly suffer. But such loss would be incidental and inevitable to any armed insurrection whatever, no matter on what principle the right of resistance should be resorted to. If he refuses, then I say—away with him—out of this land with him—himself and all his robber rights and all the things himself and his rights have brought into our island—blood and tears, and famine, and the fever that goes with famine."

In the issue of the *Irish Felon* for July 8, Lalor, expecting suppression and arrest, wrote "The Faith of a Felon"—a statement which, ill-framed and ill-connected though he knew it to be, he firmly believed to "carry the fortunes of Ireland," and sent "forth to its fate, to conquer or be conquered." It was conquered for the time, but, like such immortal things, it was destined to rise again. In it Lalor re-affirmed his principles and re-stated his programme. The idea of the ownership of the soil by the whole people, which is his essential contribution to modern political thought, was in this statement put more clearly even than before:

"What forms the right of property in land? I have never read in the direction of that question. I have all my life been destitute of books. But from the first chapter of Blackstone's second book, the only page I ever read on the subject, I know that jurists are unanimously agreed in considering 'first occupancy' to be the only true original foundation on the right of property and possession of land.

"Now, I am prepared to prove that 'occupancy' wants every character and quality that could give it moral efficacy as a foundation of right. I am prepared to prove this, when 'occupancy' has first been *defined*. If no definition can be given, I am relieved from the necessity of showing any claim founded on occupancy to be weak and worthless.

"To any plain understanding the right of private property is very simple. It is the right of man to possess, enjoy, and transfer the substance and use of whatever HE HAS HIMSELF CREATED. This title is good against the world; and it is the *sole* and *only* title by which a valid right of absolute private property can possibly vest.

"But no man can plead any such title to a right of property in the substance of the soil.

"The earth, together with all it *spontaneously* produces, is the free and common property of all mankind, of natural right, and by the grant of God—and all men being equal, no man, therefore, has a right, to appropriate exclusively to himself any part or portion thereof, except with and by the *common consent* and *agreement* of all other men.

"The sole original right of property in land which I acknowledge to be morally valid, is this right of common consent and agreement. Every other I hold to be fabricated and fictitious, null, void, and of no effect."

As for Lalor's programme of action, it was in brief:

1. To refuse all rent and arrears beyond the value of the overplus of harvest remaining after due provision for the tenants' subsistence for twelve months.

2. To resist eviction under the English law of ejection.

3. To refuse all rent to the usurping proprietors, until the people, the true proprietors, had decided in national congress what rents were to be paid, and to whom.

4. That the people should decide that rents should "be paid to *themselves*, the people, for public purposes, and for behoof and benefit of them, the entire general people."

Lalor saw clearly that this programme might, and almost certainly would, lead to armed revolution. If so—

"Welcome be the will of God. We must only try to keep our harvest, to offer a peaceful, passive resistance, to barricade the island, to break up the roads, to break down the bridges—and, should need be, and favourable occasions offer, surely we may venture to try the steel....

"It has been said to me that such a war, on the principles I propose, would be looked on with detestation by Europe. I assert the contrary. I say such a war would propagate itself throughout Europe. Mark the words of this prophecy: —The principle I propound goes to the foundations of Europe, and, sooner or later, will cause Europe to outrise. Mankind will yet be masters of the earth. The rights of the people to make the laws—this produced the first great modern earthquake, whose latest shocks, even now, are heaving in the heart of the world. The right of the people to own the land—this will produce the next. Train your hands, and your son's hands, gentlemen of earth, for you and they will yet have to use them. I want to put Ireland foremost, in the van of the world, at the head of the nations—to set her aloft in the blaze of the sun, and to make her for ages the lodestar of history. Will she take the path I point out—the path to be free, and famed, and feared, and followed—the path that goes sunward?..."

A fortnight later, in the *Irish Felon* for July 22, Lalor wrote the article "Clearing the Decks" which was intended to declare the revolution. It was worthy of a braver response than it received:

"If Ireland be conquered now—or what would be worse—if she fails to fight, it will certainly not be the fault of the people at large, of those who form the rank and file of the nation. The failure and fault will be that of those who have assumed to take the office of commanding and conducting the march of a people for liberty without, perhaps, having any commission from nature to do so, or natural right, or acquired requisite. The general population of this island are ready to find and furnish everything which can be demanded from the mass of a people—

the members, the physical strength, the animal daring, the health, hardihood, and endurance. No population on earth of equal amount would furnish a more effective military conscription. We want only competent leaders—men of courage and capacity—men whom nature meant and made for leaders.... These leaders are yet to be found. Can Ireland furnish them? It would be a sheer and absurd blasphemy against nature to doubt it. The first blow will bring them out....

"In the case of Ireland now there is but *one fact* to deal with, and *one question* to be considered. The *fact* is this—that there are at present in occupation of our country some 40,000 armed men, in the livery and service of England; and the *question* is—how best and soonest to kill and capture these 40,000?...

"Meanwhile, however, remember this—that somewhere, and somehow, and by somebody, a beginning must be made. Who strikes the first blow for Ireland? Who wins a wreath that will be green for ever?"

That was Lalor's last word. The issue containing the article was seized, the *Irish Felon* suppressed, and Martin and Lalor arrested. In a few months Lalor was released from prison a dying man. From his sick bed he tried to rally the beaten forces; he actually went down into North Munster and endeavoured to lead the people. This effort—the almost forgotten rising of 1849—failed. Lalor died in Dublin a few weeks after. But his word has marched on, conquering.

III

The doctrine and proposals of Fintan Lalor stirred John Mitchel profoundly. Mitchel was not a democrat by instinct, as Tone and Lalor were; he was not a revolutionary by process of thought, as Tone and Lalor were; he was not from the beginning of his public life a believer in the possibility and desirability of physical force, as Tone and Lalor were. He became all these things; and he became all these things suddenly. It was as if revolutionary Ireland, speaking through Lalor, had said to Mitchel, "Follow me," and Mitchel, leaving all things, followed. Duffy and others were amazed that the most conservative of the Young Irelanders should become the most revolutionary. They ought not to have been amazed. That deep and passionate man could not have been anything by halves. As well expect a Paul or a Teresa or an Ignatius Loyola to be a "moderate" Christian as John Mitchel, once that "Follow me" had been spoken, to be a "moderate" Nationalist. Mitchel was of the stuff of which the great prophets and ecstatics have been made. He did really hold converse with God; he did really deliver God's word to man, delivered it fiery-tongued.

Mitchel's is the last of the four gospels of the new testament of Irish nationality, the last and the fieriest and the most sublime. It flames with apocalyptic wrath, such wrath as there is nowhere else in literature. And it is because the man loved so well that his wrath was so terrible. It is foolish to say of Mitchel, as it has been said, that his is a gospel of hate, that hate is barren, that a nation cannot feed itself on hate without peril to its soul, or at least to the sanity and sweetness of its mind, that Davis, who preached love, is a truer leader and guide for Ireland than Mitchel, who preached hate. The answer to this is—first, that love and hate are not mutually antagonistic but mutually complementary; that love connotes hate, hate of the thing that denies or destroys or threatens the thing beloved: that love of good connotes hate of evil, love of truth hate of falsehood, love of freedom hate of oppression; that hate may be as pure and good a thing as love, just as love may be as impure and evil a thing as hate; that hate is no more ineffective and barren than love, both being as necessary to moral sanity and growth as sun and storm are to physical life and growth. And, secondly, that Mitchel, the least apologetic of men, was at pains to explain that his hate was not of English men and women, but of the English thing which called itself a government in Ireland, of the English Empire, of English commercialism supported by English militarism, a thing wholly evil, perhaps the most evil thing that there has ever been in the world. To talk of such hate as unholy, unchristian, barren, is to talk folly or hypocrisy. Such hate is not only a good thing, but is a duty.

When Mitchel's critics (or his own Doppelganger, who was his severest critic) objected that his glorious wrath was merely destructive, a thing splendid in slaying, but without any fecundity or life-giving principle within it, Mitchel's answer was adequate and conclusive:

"...Can you dare to pronounce that the winds, and the lightnings, which tear down, degrade, destroy, execute a more ignoble office than the volcanoes and subterranean deeps that upheave, renew, recreate? Are the nether fires holier than the upper fires? The waters that are above the firmament, do they hold of Ahriman, and the waters that are below the firmament, of Ormuzd? Do you take up a reproach against the lightnings for that they only shatter and shiver, but never construct? Or have you a quarrel with the winds because they fight against the churches, and build them not? In all nature, spiritual and physical, do you not see that some powers and agents have it for their function to abolish and demolish and derange—other some to construct and set in order? But is not the destruction, then, as natural, as needful, as the construction? —Rather tell me, I pray you, which is construction—which destruction? This destruction *is* creation: Death is Birth and 'The quick spring like weeds out of the dead.' Go to—the revolutionary Leveller is your only architect. Therefore, take courage, all you that Jacobins be, and stand upon your rights, and do your appointed work with all your strength, let the canting fed classes rave and shriek as they will—where you see a respectable, fair-spoken Lie sitting in high places, feeding itself fat on human sacrifices—down with it, strip it naked, and pitch it to the demons; whenever you see a greedy tyranny (constitutional or other) grinding the faces of the poor, join battle with it on the spot—conspire, confederate, and combine against it, resting never till the huge mischief come down, though the whole 'structure of society' come down along with it. Never you mind funds and stocks; if the price of the things called *Consols* depend on lies and fraud, down with them, too. Take no heed of 'social disorganisation;' you cannot bring back chaos—never fear; no disorganisation in the world can be so complete but there will be a germ of new order in it; sans-culottism, when she hath conceived, will bring forth venerable institutions. Never spare; work joyfully, according to your nature and function; and when your work is effectually done, and it is time for the counter operations to begin, why, then, you can fall a-constructing, if you have a gift that way; if not, let others do *their* work, and take your rest, having discharged your duty. Courage, Jacobins! for ye, too, are ministers of heaven....

"I do believe myself incapable of desiring private vengeance; at least, I have never yet suffered any private wrong atrocious enough to stir up that sleeping passion. The vengeance I seek is the righting of my country's wrong, which includes my own. Ireland, indeed, needs vengeance; but this is public vengeance—public justice. Herein England is truly a great public criminal. England! all England, operating through her Government; through all her organised and effectual public opinion, press, platform, pulpit, Parliament, has done, is doing, and means to do, grievous wrong to Ireland. She must be punished; that punishment will, as I believe, come upon her by and through Ireland; and so will Ireland be *avenged*."

This denunciation of woe against the enemy of Irish freedom is as necessary a part of the religion of Irish nationality as are Davis's pleas for love and concord between brother Irishmen. The Church that preaches peace and goodwill launches her anathemas against the enemies of peace and goodwill. Mitchel's gospel is part of the testament, even as Davis's is; it but reveals a different facet of the truth. A man must accept the whole testament; but a man may prefer Davis to Mitchel, just as a man may prefer the gospel according to St. Luke, the kindliest and most human of the gospels, to the gospel of St. John.

Mitchel's teaching contains nothing that is definitely new and his. He accepted Tone; he accepted Davis; he accepted in particular Lalor; and he summed up and expressed all their teaching in a language transfigured by wrath and vision. Tone is the intellectual ancestor of the whole modern movement of Irish nationalism, of Davis, and Lalor, and Mitchel, and all their followers; Davis is the immediate ancestor of the spiritual and imaginative part of that movement, embodied in our day in the Gaelic League; Lalor is the immediate ancestor of the specifically democratic part of that movement, embodied to-day in the more virile labour organisations; Mitchel is the immediate ancestor of Fenianism, the noblest and most terrible manifestation of this unconquered nation.

And just as all the four have reached, in different terms, the same gospel, making plain in turn different facets of the same truth, so the movements I have indicated are but facets of a whole, different expressions, and each one a necessary expression, of the august, though denied, truth of Irish Nationhood; nationhood in virtue of an old spiritual tradition of nationality, nationhood involving Separation and Sovereignty, nationhood resting on and guaranteeing the freedom of all the men and women of the nation and placing them in effective possession of the physical conditions necessary to the reality and to the perpetuation of their freedom, nationhood declaring and establishing and defending itself by the good smiting sword. I who have been in and of each of these movements make here the necessary synthesis, and in the name of all of them I assert the forgotten truth, and ask all who accept it to testify to it with me, here in our day and, if need be, with our blood.

At the end of a former essay I set that prophecy of Mitchel's as to the coming of a time when the kindred and tongues and nations of the earth should give their banners to the wind; and his prayer that he, John Mitchel, might live to see it, and that on that great day of the Lord he might have breath and strength enough to stand under Ireland's immortal Green. John Mitchel did not live to see it. He died, an old man, forty years before its dawning. But the day of the Lord is here, and you and I have lived to see it.

And we are young. And God has given us strength and courage and counsel. May He give us victory.

POBLACHT NA hÉIREANN

THE PROVISIONAL GOVERNMENT
OF THE
IRISH REPUBLIC
TO THE PEOPLE OF IRELAND [13]

IRISHMEN AND IRISHWOMEN: In the name of God and of the dead generations from which she receives her old tradition of nationhood, Ireland, through us, summons her children to her flag and strikes for her freedom.

Having organised and trained her manhood through her secret revolutionary organisation, the Irish Republican Brotherhood, and through her open military organisations, the Irish Volunteers and the Irish Citizen Army, having patiently perfected her discipline, having resolutely waited for the right moment to reveal itself, she now seizes that moment, and supported by her exiled children in America and by gallant allies in Europe, but relying in the first on her own strength, she strikes in full confidence of victory.

We declare the right of the people of Ireland to the ownership of Ireland and to the unfettered control of Irish destinies, to be sovereign and indefeasible. The long usurpation of that right by a foreign people and government has not extinguished the right, nor can it ever be extinguished except by the destruction of the Irish people. In every generation the Irish people have asserted their right to national freedom and sovereignty; six times during the past three hundred years they have asserted it in arms. Standing on that fundamental right and again

---

[13] Marking the beginning of the 1916 Easter Rising, Pádraic Pearse read the following Proclamation of the Republic outside the General Post Office on Sackville Street on April 24th, 1916. Though Pearse was executed on May 3rd, along with his brother and other revolutionaries of the Rising, the spirit of the Proclamation of the Republic remained, eventually culminating in an Ireland free from English rule.

asserting it in arms in the face of the world, we hereby proclaim the Irish Republic as a Sovereign Independent State, and we pledge our lives and the lives of our comrades in arms to the cause of its freedom, of its welfare, and of its exaltation among the nations.

The Irish Republic is entitled to, and hereby claims, the allegiance of every Irishman and Irishwoman. The Republic guarantees religious and civil liberty, equal rights and equal opportunities to all its citizens, and declares its resolve to pursue the happiness and prosperity of the whole nation and of all its parts, cherishing all of the children of the nation equally, and oblivious of the differences carefully fostered by an alien Government, which have divided a minority from the majority in the past.

Until our arms have brought the opportune moment for the establishment of a permanent National Government, representative of the whole people of Ireland and elected by the suffrages of all her men and women, the Provisional Government, hereby constituted, will administer the civil and military affairs of the Republic in trust for the people.

We place the cause of the Irish Republic under the protection of the Most High God, Whose blessing we invoke upon our arms, and we pray that no one who serves that cause will dishonour it by cowardice, inhumanity, or rapine. In this supreme hour the Irish nation must, by its valour and discipline, and by the readiness of its children to sacrifice themselves for the common good, prove itself worthy of the august destiny to which it is called.

Signed on behalf of the Provisional Government:

THOMAS J. CLARKE,

SEÁN Mac DIARMADA,   THOMAS MacDONAGH,

P. H. PEARSE,   ÉAMONN CEANNT,

JAMES CONNOLLY,   JOSEPH PLUNKETT.

SELECT POEMS

THE FOOL

THE REBEL

THE MOTHER

THE WAYFARER

THE FOOL

Written after the death of dear friend and Fenian Jeremiah O'Donovan Rossa, who died in late June 1915, this poem was released by Pearse after Rossa's funeral in August 1915.

Since the wise men have not spoken, I speak that am only a fool;

A fool that hath loved his folly,

Yea, more than the wise men their books or their counting houses or
their quiet homes,

Or their fame in men's mouths;

A fool that in all his days hath done never a prudent thing,

Never hath counted the cost, nor recked if another reaped

The fruit of his mighty sowing, content to scatter the seed;

A fool that is unrepentant, and that soon at the end of all

Shall laugh in his lonely heart as the ripe ears fall to the reaping-hooks

And the poor are filled that were empty,

Tho' he go hungry.

I have squandered the splendid years that the Lord God gave to my
youth

In attempting impossible things, deeming them alone worth the toil.

Was it folly or grace? Not men shall judge me, but God.

I have squandered the splendid years:

Lord, if I had the years I would squander them over again,

Aye, fling them from me!

For this I have heard in my heart, that a man shall scatter, not hoard,

Shall do the deed of to-day, nor take thought of tomorrow's teen,

Shall not bargain or huxter with God; or was it a jest of Christ's

And is this my sin before men, to have taken Him at His word?

The lawyers have sat in council, the men with the keen, long faces,

And said, 'This man is a fool,' and others have said, 'He blasphemeth;'

And the wise have pitied the fool that hath striven to give a life

In the world of time and space among the bulks of actual things,

To a dream that was dreamed in the heart, and that only the heart could
hold.

O wise men, riddle me this: what if the dream come true?

What if the dream come true? and if millions unborn shall dwell

In the house that I shaped in my heart, the noble house of my thought?

Lord, I have staked my soul, I have staked the lives of my kin

On the truth of Thy dreadful word. Do not remember my failures,

But remember this my faith

And so I speak.

Yea, ere my hot youth pass, I speak to my people and say:

Ye shall be foolish as I; ye shall scatter, not save;

Ye shall venture your all, lest ye lose what is more than all;

Ye shall call for a miracle, taking Christ at His word.

And for this I will answer, O people, answer here and hereafter,

O people that I have loved, shall we not answer together?

THE REBEL

Written in 1915, this poem inspired Pearse's compatriots to action in the Easter Rising of 1916, the revolt for which he was executed.

I am come of the seed of the people, the people that sorrow;

Who have no treasure but hope,

No riches laid up but a memory

Of an ancient glory.

My mother bore me in bondage, in bondage my mother was born,

I am of the blood of serfs;

The children with whom I have played, the men and women with
    whom I have eaten

Have had masters over them, have been under the lash of masters,

And though gentle, have served churls.

The hands that have touched mine, the dear hands whose touch is
    familiar to me,

Have worn shameful manacles, have been bitten at the wrist by
    manacles,

Have grown hard with the manacles and the task-work of strangers,

I am flesh of the flesh of these lowly, I am bone of their bone

I that have never submitted;

I that have a soul greater than the souls of my people's masters,

I that have vision and prophecy, and the gift of fiery speech,

I that have spoken with God on top of His holy hill.

And because I am of the people, I understand the people,

I am sorrowful with their sorrow, I am hungry with their desire;

My heart has been heavy with the grief of mothers,

My eyes have been wet with the tears of children,

I have yearned with old wistful men

And laughed or cursed with young men;

Their shame is my shame, and I have reddened for it,

Reddened for that they have served, they who should be free,

Reddened for that they have gone in want, while others have been full,

Reddened for that they have walked in fear of lawyers and of their
jailers

With their Writs of Summons and their handcuffs,

Men mean and cruel!

I could have borne stripes on my body rather than this shame of my
people.

And now I speak, being full of vision;

I speak to my people, and I speak in my people's name to the masters
of my people.

I say to my people that they are holy, that they are august, despite their
chains,

That they are greater than those that hold them, and stronger and purer,

That they have but need of courage, and to call on the names of their
God,

God the unforgetting, the dear God that loves the peoples

For whom He died naked, suffering shame.

And I say to my people's masters: Beware,

Beware of the thing that is coming, beware of the risen people

Who shall take what ye would not give.

Did ye think to conquer the people,

Or that Law is stronger than life and than men's desire to be free?

We will try it out with you, ye that have harried and held,

Ye that have bullied and bribed, tyrants, hypocrites, liars!

THE MOTHER

Written in May 1916 as he awaited execution in Kilmainham Gaol, this poem was mentioned by Pearse in his final letter to his mother, dated May 3rd, the day of his execution: "You asked me to write a little poem which would seem to be said by you about me. I have written it, and a copy is in Arbour Hill Barracks with other papers and Father Aloysius is taking care of another copy of it."

I do not grudge them: Lord, I do not grudge
My two strong sons that I have seen go out
To break their strength and die, they and a few,
In bloody protest for a glorious thing,
They shall be spoken of among their people,
The generations shall remember them,
And call them blessed;
But I will speak their names to my own heart
In the long nights;
The little names that were familiar once
Round my dead hearth.
Lord, thou art hard on mothers:
We suffer in their coming and their going;
And tho' I grudge them not, I weary, weary
Of the long sorrow - And yet I have my joy:
My sons were faithful, and they fought.

THE WAYFARER

Written on the eve of his execution in May 1916, this final poem by Pearse serves as his final statement.

The beauty of the world hath made me sad,

This beauty that will pass;

Sometimes my heart hath shaken with great joy

To see a leaping squirrel in a tree,

Or a red lady-bird upon a stalk,

Or little rabbits in a field at evening,

Lit by a slanting sun,

Or some green hill where shadows drifted by

Some quiet hill where mountainy man hath sown

And soon would reap; near to the gate of Heaven;

Or children with bare feet upon the sands

Of some ebbed sea, or playing on the streets

Of little towns in Connacht,

Things young and happy.

And then my heart hath told me:

These will pass,

Will pass and change, will die and be no more,

Things bright and green, things young and happy;

And I have gone upon my way

Sorrowful.